The Journal of Hildegard of Bingen

The Journal of Hildegard of Bingen

A NOVEL BY

BARBARA LACHMAN

Bell Tower New York

Grateful acknowledgment is made to the following for permission to reprint: Bear & Company for excerpts from *Hildegard of Bingen's Book of Divine Works* edited by Matthew Fox. Copyright © 1987 by Bear & Company, Inc.; E. J. Brill for excerpts from *Fabula: Explorations into the Uses of Myth in Medieval Platonism* by Peter Dronke. Copyright © 1974 by E. J. Brill; Cambridge University Press for excerpts from *Women Writers of the Middle Ages* by Peter Dronke. Copyright © 1984 by Cambridge University Press; Paulist Press for excerpts from *Hildegard of Bingen: Scivias* translated by Mother Columba Hart and Jane Bishop. Copyright © 1990 by Paulist Press; University of California Press for excerpts from *Sister of Wisdom: St. Hildegard's Theology of the Feminine* by Barbara Newman. Copyright © 1987 by The Regents of the University of California; Yale University Press for excerpts from *The Old English Advent* by Robert Burlin. Copyright © 1968 by Yale University Press.

Published by Bell Tower, an imprint of Harmony Books, a division of Crown Publishers, Inc., 201 East 50th Street, New York, New York 10022. Member of the Crown Publishing Group. Random House, Inc. New York, Toronto, London, Sydney, Auckland.

Bell Tower and colophon are registered trademarks of Crown Publishers, Inc.

Manufactured in the United States of America

Library of Congress Cataloging-in-Publication Data

Lachman, Barbara.
   The journal of Hildegard of Bingen/by Barbara Lachman.
      p. cm.
   Includes bibliographical references.
   1. Hildegard, Saint, 1098-1179—Fiction. 2. Germany—History—843-1273—Fiction.
3. Christian saints—Germany—Fiction.
I. Title.
PS3562.A244J68 1993
813'.54—dc20
                                  92-40768
                                  CIP

ISBN 0-517-59169-3

10 9 8 7 6 5 4 3 2 1

First Edition

Contents

Acknowledgments

Since this project has, in one form or another, been an essential focus of my life for so many years, one of its unlooked-for rewards has been the discovery and deepening of friendships with remarkable women who offered belief and encouragement in the work, whether it was in the form of musical performances, collective writing projects, work-in-progress conferences, or the many other innovative ways that women have discovered to support and genuinely participate in one another's work. To each of these particular women, my heartfelt gratitude.

A few people who cheerfully answered strange inquiries for information in ways that surprised me are Hugo Feiss, OSB, Ron Shouldice at the Bio-dynamic Farming and Gardening Association, and Dames Hildelith and Margaret at Stanbrook Abbey in England.

Particular thanks to Janet Levy, who was an early sympathetic reader and pushed my manuscript in the right direction;

to Barbara Newman, who has seen a few stages of this work and whose extraordinary range of scholarship and incisive humor-about-the-world continue to inspire me;

to Toinette Lippe, my editor and the founder of this singular imprint, who was able to see both the forest and the trees, and whose tireless patient attention has never waned; and

to John Blackley, without whose persistent devotion I would not be a writer, who read every draft from the first, and served as in-house liturgist and architect of the glossary.

Preface

Hildegard of Bingen (1098–1179) lived in the Rhineland as a monastic in a cloister, obedient to the Benedictine Rule, for seventy-three of her eighty-one years. In her forty-third year she began to record visions she had received since earliest childhood; once begun, her creative output never stopped, in spite of her gender, poor health, lack of formalized schooling, and the intermittent but intimidating opposition of a male hierarchy. She received visions that illuminated the deepest meanings of religious texts and events, and produced poetry and music for at least seventy-seven liturgical songs and the first morality play, a compendium of the healing arts as she practiced them, and a descriptive catalog of flora and fauna of the natural world. She responded to well over 150 letters from people of Church and State seeking her advice, largely about matters of authority and responsibility; she founded and ruled as abbess an autonomous community of Benedictine nuns and, eventually, a second daughter house nearby.

For more than seven hundred years, all this work remained virtually unknown outside Germany: Her writings were available in Latin only, two attempts at official canonization had failed (although she is remembered as a saint in her own country), and she was known to a small portion of the English-speaking world, by reputation only, as an obscure prophetess with the catchy title "Sybil of the Rhine." Hildegard began to emerge from obscurity in Europe, where Benedictine nuns of the former daughter house in Eibingen were among the first to undertake the translation of her works into German; by the late 1960s this project was almost complete. Peter Dronke's pioneering work in England revealed an early appreciation of the extraordinary depth and originality of her thinking, and English translations of her major works have been published in the last decade.

In the United States, the attention of medievalists was directed first to her visions and eventually to her music, which recordings have at last made accessible. Now that she has our ears, we are amazed that her exemplary life and artistic achievements could have been ignored for so long: Women especially find themselves enormously drawn to her for inspiration. But attempts to turn Hildegard into a feminist can be misleading. She believed that women were inherently weaker than men, and everything she accomplished was predicated on devoting her sexuality to Christ. Not only did she accept inequality between the sexes and between classes, but she was absolute ruler of the women, lands, and animals in her care in a way that we in the twentieth century would identify as a hallmark of the patriarchal household. On the other hand, if living the life of a feminist means "to articulate a self-consciousness about women's identity both as inherited cultural fact and as process of social construction,"* then Hildegard was indeed a pioneering feminist.

She also speaks directly to a crisis peculiar to our time: Now that we have gone to such pains to translate, demystify, analyze, and explain everything from the raising of children to the evolution of the earth and its inhabitants, and have technologically replicated the means of sexual reproduction as well as the process of musical composition, mystery itself seems to have vanished from the culture. Hildegard reminds us that the material world is filled with wonders we can see but not fully comprehend, that the body can be afflicted by sicknesses and torments only the spirit can heal. If it is true that gods and goddesses manifest in

---

*Part of a definition by Nancy K. Miller, quoted in Carolyn Heilbrun's *Writing a Woman's Life*, New York: W.W. Norton, 1987, p. 18.

new forms when great need arises, the groundswell of interest in Hildegard of Bingen may serve such an epiphany. It is in this understanding that I have sought her, certain that she has singular things to tell us, of a very practical nature, about the conditions for creativity.

The more I have learned during the last twenty years about Hildegard of Bingen's human limitations—her never-ending skirmishes with ill health, her restless determination to overreach herself, and her self-admitted depressive temperament—the more mysterious to me are the range and depth of her accomplishments as a woman in the twelfth century. Since Latin was then the universal language of learning throughout Christendom, I relearned Latin in order to study her writings in the original and learned medieval neumatic notation in order to appreciate the striking originality of her musical compositions. According to her own notes, letters, and the correspondence of her contemporaries, Hildegard's skill as a healer and her empirical knowledge about the medicinal use of plants, diet, and attitude were remarkably well known in her lifetime, and so I studied for three years and have practiced for ten a traditional technique utilizing the laying on of hands in order to understand more fully the relationship between subtle energies in the body and deep, concentrated intentions of the mind. I have read about her, sung her music, and dreamed of her.

Insofar as Hildegard has revealed herself to me, I have recorded these journal entries, mainly for Sundays, when the work periods in a medieval monastery were most forgiving. I chose the year 1152 because of the unrelenting obstacles it presented to this abbess, who had had the vision and audacity less than two years earlier to win the right to lead a community of nuns to independence from the male monastery in which they had always had their physical home, economic support, and spiritual direction. After ascertaining the date of Easter, I worked out the corresponding dates for the movable feasts for the complete liturgical year. In recording Hildegard's journal, I read the same 150 psalms she sang each week, used the same Vulgate version of the Bible she knew, and read the sermons and other writings of the great Church Fathers that she and her nuns chanted during the long night office of Matins.

In all my activity I have, like Hildegard, observed prolonged periods of silence, most especially but not always during flare-ups of chronic illness. I have waited impatiently, and listened. I urge readers to read the journal entries aloud to themselves with moving lips, in the same way that words were always read in the twelfth century. My hope is that the entries can be read, heard, and experienced without critical notes. For those unfamiliar with Benedictine life in the Middle Ages, there are explanations of some basic terms, definitions, and practices in a glossary at the very end of the book. Names of historical people and places in the text are identified in brief notes or commentaries on the pages where they occur; characters and events that are not identified in this way have their source in my own spiritual experience. This is a kind of knowledge which was very familiar to Hildegard of Bingen.

Chronology of Hildegard's Life
1098–1151

1098   The last of ten children, Hildegard was born to a noble German family in Bermersheim, not far from Mainz.

1106   Jutta, daughter of Count von Sponheim, took the vow of anchoress, or recluse, housed and fed by the male monastery of Disibodenberg; Hildegard's parents entrusted her care and upbringing to Jutta.

1106–   A few other women joined Jutta's hermitage, forming a small enclosed
1136   community living according to the Rule of St. Benedict within the walls of Disibodenberg, and obedient to Abbot Kuno. At age fourteen or fifteen, Hildegard was formally professed a Benedictine nun.

1136   At the death of Jutta, Hildegard was elected to lead the community of women.

1141   Hildegard was summoned in a vision to "tell and write" what she "saw and heard" in her visions; frightening periods of illness recurred. Her confessor and priest, Volmar, and a sister nun, Rikkarda von Stade, provided moral support, and Hildegard began writing.

1141–   With Volmar as secretary, Hildegard recorded her first book of
1151   visions, eventually entitled *Scivias*. The last of these visions includes the texts of fourteen liturgical songs composed by Hildegard as well as a rudimentary version of what eventually became her *Ordo virtutum* (Play of the Virtues), a sung morality play and the earliest of its type. In 1146 or 1147 Hildegard, in a letter to Bernard of Clairvaux, sought confirmation of the prophetic call that prompted her to write.

1147–
1148
At the synod of Trier, on the recommendation of Bernard and the archbishop of Mainz, Pope Eugenius III reviewed a portion of the *Scivias* with the synod members. They confirmed the truth of the work, and the pope sent a letter of apostolic blessing and protection to Hildegard at Disibodenberg. Hildegard determined to establish an independent convent for her women—an anomaly—and received visions supporting its establishment on a desolate mountain containing ruins of a ninth-century religious foundation of St. Rupert. The monks of Disibodenberg, led by Abbot Kuno, opposed the move. Hildegard sought help from Archbishop Henry of Mainz and Marchioness Richardis von Stade. Because of the conflict, Hildegard experienced paralyzing illness, witnessed by Abbot Kuno, which miraculously abated when consent was given.

1148
With the purchase of the land, construction was begun at Rupertsberg. Relying on gifts of land and the transference of dowries already given by the families of her nuns, Hildegard initiated a protracted struggle for her community's economic and spiritual independence.

1150
Hildegard and twenty nuns moved to Rupertsberg, where she served as abbess. Volmar, Hildegard's trusted secretary-scribe and the priest necessary for celebrating Mass, was the only man to accompany them.

The Journal of Hildegard of Bingen

The last vision was more like a visitation, it was so fleeting; simple, direct, and wordless in the few seconds I allowed for contemplation. Outside the casement I saw the broad sycamore once again shorn of leaves, its branches grappling the winter sky, its base solidly in the earth. Suddenly the tree began physically to move in the quiet light of midday. Its motion seemed such that I and everything I knew or could imagine was present in that tree and shared the same fluid, energetic breathing. The privileged glimpse was gone in a moment, though I have no doubt the joyous movement continues still. I crave its beauty like food, but it is so difficult to maintain a contemplative state when the responsibility for the music of both Mass and Office rests entirely in my lap.[1] Thank God for the bells, the protection of the *Ave Maria*,[2] the calls to prayer, the assurance of

■ 1. Monastic life revolved around the Mass or Eucharist (giving thanks), by which the death and resurrection of Christ were ritually made present. Collections of psalms and liturgical texts sung eight times each day—the Divine Office, or *opus dei* (the work of God)—served as a setting for the Mass and a means whereby the Eucharistic presence continued from morning into the night.

■ 2. Recitation of the *Ave Maria* (Hail Mary), based on the greeting of the angel Gabriel to the Virgin Mary in Luke 1:42, was used from medieval times in Germany. The prayer would be repeated each evening to the tolling of a bell, the same bell that summoned the monastic community from manual labor, study, silence, or sleep to Mass and to each of the eight sung offices.

I

privacy, the practice of our vows, the familiarity and friendly, consistent demands of the Rule.[3] If only my raw-from-the-world recruits could see these as blessings that grace the monastic life and loosen the fierce attachments that restrict us!

Public responsibilities cloud my inner life until it is nearly invisible. This is the second full year of pleading and arguing, negotiating for new lands, transferring dowries from Disibodenberg against the wishes of my old Abbot Kuno, and always at the expense of my frail health; protection of the archbishop at Mainz is secured, permission for my writing to continue is granted through the Cistercian pope with the support of Br. Bernard of Clairvaux,[4] but with each day here, the responsibilities multiply. My head is constantly crowded, crawling with petty details of food and supplies, programs of instruction for the novices, decisions to be made at every juncture for the building of the cloister church.

And how can I ignore the letters? People find me here; they seek me out, in need of advice and encour-

3. The Benedictine Rule was set down in the 6th century by Benedict of Nursia, for the monastery he founded in Monte Cassino, Italy; it became the prevalent rule for monastic communities throughout Western Europe by the end of the 8th century, and it is still used by Benedictine communities today. The Rule prescribes in remarkable detail a particularly balanced regimen for life in a community where the singing of the Divine Office is the central work. Stability of residence, obedience, and conversion (of fear into love) are required, and these join the ubiquitous gospel counsels of poverty and chastity.

4. Several years after she had begun writing down her first book of visions, called *Scivias* (an abbreviated and cryptic Latin word meaning "to know the ways of the Lord"), Hildegard wrote to the influential Cistercian monk, Bernard of Clairvaux (Epistle 29 in J. P. Migne, *Patrologia Latina*, vol. 197, Paris: 1855 [hereinafter *PL*], pp. 189–90). At that time, Bernard was abbot of Cîteaux, the motherhouse of the Cistercian order, which was a relatively new, highly successful but extremely austere reform of Benedictine monasticism.

agement, and even dear Volmar's willingness to record whatever I dictate doesn't relieve me of the responsibility to answer each one.[5] The whole body of Advent music lies before us, and I am the only one who knows it and therefore must teach it. Underneath it all, I am plagued by the desire to begin as soon as possible on music for all of the offices for the Feast of St. Ursula.[6] It is early yet, but by next October I pray that we can honor her with music of our own, because a vision as strong as hers will inspire my women to go beyond their grumblings and limitations. The music comes when it will come, and I must find a way to stay open to it in the midst of all the chaos.

Two extremes tempt me these days: One is a deep

⬧ 5. Against the objections of Abbot Kuno, Hildegard brought Volmar with her to serve as priest in her community's new home on Mount St. Rupert. He was Hildegard's scribe from the first recording of her *Scivias* at Disibodenberg until his death in 1173. After her prophetic gift had been officially recognized, Hildegard received and answered nearly three hundred letters; very few have been translated from Latin into English. Her correspondents ranged from popes, archbishops, bishops, emperors, kings, abbots, abbesses, and prioresses to many secular and religious petitioners who were sufficiently learned and thoughtful to seek her advice, prayers, and wisdom.

⬧ 6. The Feast of St. Ursula & the 11,000 Virgins was celebrated throughout the Western Church on October 21. Her story, known primarily through the many reprintings of *The Golden Legend* of Jacobus Voragine, memorializes the life, vision, pilgrimage, and passion (martyrdom) of a Christian princess and her band of virgin followers; we also know it through the inspired paintings of Memling and Carpaccio. The story is based on an ancient Roman inscription in Cologne, which testifies to the fact that a small group of Christian virgins was martyred there, perhaps by marauding Huns, in the 4th century. (The 11,000 Virgins is a scribal error; early in the transmission of the legend, someone mistakenly transcribed the Latin *XI MV* as "*XI mille* [thousand] *virgines*" instead of "*XI martyres virgines*".) Although the Church was from the first skeptical of Ursula's story and has long since eliminated all of the specific music for the Mass and

longing for the simplicity, the real anonymity and isolation of my long novitiate with Blessed Jutta at Disibodenberg; the other, the brilliance of the ecstatic state—allowing myself to be taken over by such powerful inner sights and sounds that I would be forced to give up my shepherding of these women for stretches of time and lose contact with the sensory world altogether.[7] But not today. The Season of the Coming is upon us. It is the first of a new liturgical year, and—like any birth—Advent and labor are intractable once begun: I must do all.

December 8, 1151
Second Sunday in Advent

Sometimes I am so hopeful, so filled with the light of Christ, and some days I think my women understand nothing. Volmar tells me that the *ordo* of the Mass this morning was in jeopardy, because Gertrudis, my sacristan, was so distracted she neglected to bring the bread from the bakehouse for consecration. Who here really knows enough to be

Office of her feast, her importance in the minds of medieval and Renaissance painters, hagiographers, and believers was beyond mere reason. During Hildegard's lifetime the great zeal for St. Ursula intensified; her story elaborated and spread. In 1106, workmen, enlarging the walls around the city of Cologne, struck what must have been an ancient Roman burial ground right outside the Church of St. Ursula, and the belief was that the bones found there were those of Ursula and her followers. This seemed such powerful physical evidence that the bones were sought by individual parishes and communities throughout Europe, and often housed in artistically exquisite reliquaries. Ursula was undoubtedly Hildegard's most important role model. Out of a total of seventy-seven songs written for liturgical use, thirteen were written for the Feast of St. Ursula, clearly out of all proportion to the honor she gave to any of the other saints on the calendar. The author's translations of the Ursula songs from the Latin may be found in the Appendix.

7. Only once, in the writing of her last book of visions, the *Liber divinorum operum* (Book of the Divine Works), did Hildegard in fact allow herself to enter the ecstatic state. For the rest, she says, "Truly I saw these visions not in

sacristan besides Rikkarda, who's already my prioress?[8] And Volmar, my poor priest. After all my successful pleading with Abbot Kuno to bring Volmar with us to Rupertsberg, I begin to realize it is I who have the ultimate responsibility for teaching them how to order their lives. He celebrates our Mass with such great beauty; he still finds time to encourage me to dictate to him. He knows that even though the *Scivias* visions are recorded at last, there is more for me to write besides letters.[9]

But even my dear Volmar must not teach them the Divine Office or the arrangement of the calendar, to say nothing of the meaning of that calendar: the successions and fulfilments of one Season by another, the glorious tension between a specifically dated and fixed feast, such as a saint's day, and a feast like Pen-

dreams, neither in sleep nor in ecstatic trance, neither with human bodily eyes or external ears, nor did I sense them by withdrawing myself to hidden places; rather did I willingly receive them—vigilantly, considering them carefully, in clear thought according to the will of God, in open, accessible places with my human interior eyes and ears." (*PL*, p. 348) Translations from the Latin are the author's throughout, unless otherwise indicated.

✛ 8. Rikkarda, who had been with Hildegard at Disibodenberg and was her favorite, was daughter of the Marchioness von Stade, whose wealth and influence helped Hildegard to establish her convent at Rupertsberg. In 1151, Rikkarda was unexpectedly called to be abbess at Bassum. This was probably engineered by her brother Hartwig, then the ambitious archbishop of Bremen. The appointment was in violation of the Benedictine promise of stability and was bitterly opposed by Hildegard, who expressed her views in strongly worded letters to Rikkarda's mother the marchioness, to her brother Hartwig, to Henry the archbishop of Mainz, and even to Pope Eugenius III.

✛ 9. Hildegard's creative output during the first years at Rupertsberg is staggering, even by modern, computer-day standards. In addition to the ever-growing volume of correspondence, she composed at least seventy-seven liturgical songs and the sung morality play *Ordo virtutum* (Order of the Virtues). These were gathered into a cycle entitled *Symphonia harmoniae celestium revelationum*

tecost, that moves with the Season and may therefore intersect with the other in a way that comments anew on the meaning of both. That is my job, and it is time to begin in earnest, now that we have divided our space and created enough physical order to attend to our real work, the singing of the Divine Office. My sisters in Christ will learn by doing. They will sing eight offices a day without fail, and the order and design will begin to emerge for them from the blessed dailiness of the singing. Singing the psalms in their ritual order each week will bring a knowledge that is not easily forgotten![10]

It is clear that music—singing the offices and listening to the sacred texts, even adding some new music of my own—is my best hope for teaching. At the same time, I must attend my own visions and dare to bring forth again what music God sends to this new-born community through gifts inhabiting my own frail form. It is the Virgin whose antiphons present themselves to me most often; it is She who is singing in my inner ear. Men who survive and return from the Holy Jer-

(Symphony of the Harmony of Celestial Revelations). During the same period, she was compiling two very different works that grew out of her knowledge and practice of healing. One, known to us as *Physica* (Natural History or Book of Simple Medicine) is divided into nine sections that name and describe the qualities of plants, trees, precious stones, fish, birds, animals, reptiles, metals, and three out of the four elements. In the second work, known as *Causae et curae* (Causes and Cures or Book of Compound Medicine), Hildegard categorizes specific physiological and psychological temperaments of human beings, addresses particular problems of women such as menstruation and gestation, and prescribes in detail the uses of specific plants, precious stones, prayers, and charms for certain common ailments, the latter also taking into account her received knowledge and some original ideas about astrology and cosmology. Neither of these works is yet available in English translation.

10. Hildegard's nuns sang all 150 psalms of the Old Testament each week, not in numerical order but divided unevenly among the eight offices and according to specific days of the week.

usalem War say that in the East She is called *Theotokos*, Mother of God.[11] Surely Theotokos, Mother of God and Most Blessed Virgin, will guide us as a new order of virgins. We are still so freshly in this spot on the Rupertsberg: yet untried as a productive Benedictine community, but already survivors of a privation and physical hardship previously unknown to most of the noblewomen in my care.

So many are errant and headstrong and require the limits of my patience in shepherding, that my sleep is terrible. This morning I woke long before dawn, well before the first bell for Lauds. (At least the bells ring now; that in itself signals progress, because last year during Advent we could not hope for such regularity. Our new bell had not even been cast, and my own voice was a hoarse instrument calling them to prayer.) Accompanying the cry of the earliest rooster, I heard with my inner ear the trumpeting of the antiphon for the Christmas Magnificat:[12] ‡‡ *Today the Christ is born, today a savior has appeared; today on earth angels are singing, archangels rejoicing; today the righteous*

11. "Holy Jerusalem War" is Hildegard's way of referring to the Crusades, a term not in use before the 13th century. The Second Crusade was begun in 1147 and vigorously promoted by Bernard of Clairvaux, among others. The rationale behind all the Crusades was the importance of the experience of pilgrimage to Jerusalem and other holy places sanctified by the life and teachings of Christ. This rationale was given support by an ecclesiastical decree that anyone who gave his life to defend the holy places for Christianity achieved the status of martyr in the Church. The Greek name *Theotokos* has always been retained in the Eastern rite to refer to the Virgin Mary.

12. The text of the Magnificat (Luke 1:46–55) begins,

> *My soul doth magnify the Lord*
> *And my spirit hath rejoiced in God my Savior*
> *Because he has regarded the humility of his handmaid,*
> *For behold from henceforth all generations shall call*
>   *me blessed.*

This New Testament canticle is sung each day at the office of Vespers, and its text never varies. An antiphon is a brief text sung before and after the canticles and psalms in the Divine Office; these change each day according to the

exult and say, Glory to God in the highest, alleluia![13]‡‡ Mother of God, this morning the herald of that glorious antiphon reminded me only that by this eighth day of Advent, the Season of the Coming is already well upon us. Before we know it, we will be pulled headlong into the final week of Advent, with its seven great antiphons encircling the Magnificat canticle each day, so deeply engraved in my soul. Each of their texts is more expectant and lucently beautiful than the next, and they in turn bring us almost without rest to the moment of the birth itself: Christmas Vespers and Matins, the delivery, and our deliverance through Christ in His Nativity. Only once before have we sung these "O Antiphons" in our own home, our own community and choir, with their direct, beseeching openings that thrust us into liturgical time.

But in this, our second year of Advent at Rupertsberg, my women need to understand a further meaning of the Season. This time at Advent we both initiate and complete the temporal cycle of the liturgical year with our praises for the hope of the world. In the larger sense of time, they must understand and celebrate not only the coming of Christ at His birth, but also the coming of Christ at the end of time—the Parousia! Gospel texts of "the last things," of the destruction of the temple, suggest this understanding,[14] but they hardly grasp the enormity of the Second Coming, the way that all things shall be fulfilled and made right, even taking us back to Paradise and the

particular feast and Season and have as their purpose the focusing of the worshippers' minds and hearts. The antiphon Hildegard heard is sung only once each year and is therefore "proper" to the Vespers for the Feast of the Nativity (Christmas).

❧ 13. *Hodie christus natus est: hodie salvator apparuit: hodie in terra canunt angeli, laetantur archangeli: hodie exultant justi, dicentes: gloria in excelsis deo, alleluia.*

❧ 14. The Gospels of the Masses for the last Sunday after Pentecost and the succeeding First Sunday in Advent (Matthew 24:15–35 and Luke 21:25–33, respectively) pointedly refer to the chaos that will signal the end of time and precede the Second Coming of Christ.

Tree of Life, righting, through the womb of the Virgin, the loss of eternity in the Garden.[15]

They need so much education that I am sometimes seized by melancholy. And my own needs are not simple; if I wait, the Virgin inevitably appears to me, sometimes subsumed in the sparkling sapphire figure of Sapientia,[16] surrounded by the embracing circles of infused light that both support her weight in gravity and themselves wheel around her as the form of the living movement of the Trinity, as it moves in the world. Sometimes she appears monumental and iconic, as Ecclesia, towering over the earth in cosmic proportions that dwarf our poor, womanly forms.[17] Though frail, new, and untried, we seem to be struggling into a new possibility of service as women, extending the hope of the

15. Hildegard's persistent understanding that not only Christ but Mary herself has a role in restoring the world to its state of perpetual *viriditas* (greenness) and immortality is supported by the Biblical passage from Genesis 3:15–16, in which God speaks to the serpent: "I will put enmity between thee and the woman, and thy seed and her seed: she shall crush thy head, and thou shalt lie in wait for her heel." Historically, this text quickly took on a messianic interpretation, in which Mary, as the second Eve, crushes the serpent through the fruit of her womb, destroying evil and—by extension—death. This kind of interpretation, like the wordplay between Ave (Ave Maria) and Eva (Latin for Eve) was especially beloved by medieval Biblical commentators, who believed that virtually everything in the Old Testament found its meaning as a prefigurement of events in the New Testament.

16. Hildegard has both an intimate and a mystical relationship with *Sapientia* (Wisdom), the female figure in the Bible who "was with God from the beginning" and figures predominantly in the Books of Proverbs, Wisdom, and Ecclesiasticus. For Hildegard, it is invariably the "Voice of Wisdom" that interprets her visions, assigning complex meanings to all of the colorful details.

17. Ecclesia, or *Mater ecclesia* (Mother Church) is, according to mystical Church doctrine, the "bride of Christ." As she appears in Hildegard's visions, Ecclesia is sometimes conflated with the Virgin Mary, sometimes

world in what emerge increasingly as womanish times, since clerics neglect their duties, preoccupied by worldly ambitions. But it is not only clerics, because even our Benedictine brothers become less attendant upon the *opus dei,* the singing of the Divine Office, as they become busy with the duties that follow from their seemingly inevitable ordination as priests. Our voices and prayers are needed in such a void, and we inherit a particular role in the history of salvation as an order of virgins intent on more authentically carrying the monastic way of life forward into these new times.

And so it is fitting that we pointedly honor the Blessed Virgin at the climax of Advent. On the Eve of Christmas, preceding the *"Hodie christus natus est"* I heard with the roosters this morning, we will this year announce both the Birth and the Parousia through the womb that incarnates Him in a new, more specific antiphon for Her Magnificat: At First Vespers on the Eve I will myself intone *"Hodie aperuit"* as the antiphon for Our Lady:

> *Today the closed gate has opened to us,*
> *because the serpent has suffocated*
>   *in the woman.*
> *Therefore the flower of the Virgin Mary*
>   *radiates illuminated in the first blush of daybreak.*[18]

This honors Her at the birthing of Her Son, framing with a new song the ordinary Magnificat that we sing with Her each day of the year. The more we contact Her real presence, the greater our strength on this mountain.

with Sapientia. In the arresting opening of Hildegard's Sequence for St. Ursula, Ecclesia is portrayed as a towering female figure lifted right out of the Song of Songs:

> *O Ecclesia, your eyes are like sapphire,*
> *Your ears like the mountain of Bethel;*
> *Your nose is a column of incense and myrrh,*
> *And your mouth is the sound of abundant waters.*

18. *Hodie aperuit nobis clausa porta, quod serpens in*

Volmar's visitor from Anglia tells him that in the great house of St. Gall,[19] where he has stayed at length, the monks sing additional "O Antiphons" while processing to the cross during those last pressing days of Advent. A waiting dance of sorts while singing the best of them—"*O virgo virginum*," "*O domina mundi*," "*O Jerusalem*."[20] To process for solemn feasts is part of the journey, the monastic pilgrimage that is open to women. When they write to me, the abbesses and *dominae*, complaining of restlessness, the need to travel, the desire for Jerusalem, to go to the holy places and see the Church of the Holy Sepulchre, the Mount of Olives, to fast where Christ fed the multitude, I sense they are tired of shepherding their own meager flocks, starving for nourishment, and in need of obedience that is meaningful.

The notion of "*domina mundi*" is

December 25, 1151
Feast of the Nativity

muliere suffocavit. Unde lucet in aurora flos de virgine maria. (For Latin text and music in Gregorian choral notation, see #6 in Barth, Ritscher, and Schmidt-Georg, *Hildegard von Bingen Lieder*, Salzburg, 1969 [hereinafter *Lieder*], p. 218.) With the "*Hodie apparuit*" (Today is opened) Hildegard paraphrases the "*Hodie...apparuit*" (Today...has appeared) of the antiphon quoted on p. 8; the one refers to Christ, Hildegard's to His Mother. In the ever-growing number of popular sequences written for the Virgin during the 11th and 12th centuries, *clausa porta* (the closed gate) became one of Her most important attributes; in a sense, it became a kind of metonymic phrase for the whole mystery of Christ's virgin birth. The "closed gate" as embodied in Mary becomes the intact vagina behind which lies the womb-garden that only the King may enter. This numinous meaning of *clausa porta* stems from the vision of Ezekiel in 44:1–3, where it represents the holy of holies.

19. Benedictine monastery in Switzerland, named after the 7th-century Irish missionary Gallus. Its 9th-century scriptorium, to which manuscripts were brought from all over Europe for copying, produced an extensive library which is still in existence there today.

20. In 12th-century monastic and cathedral centers, the final week of the Advent Season—that unique mixture

open to all of us.[21] The hoped-for journey to Jerusalem, the long route to Compostela,[22] the mountainous crossing to Rome are ours for meditation and inspiration. Processing from one holy spot to another in our new cloister church will illuminate and specifically mark those places where our feet will tread again and again.

The Christmas Matins are endless, and only by starting in the middle of the night could we have managed it at all. Rendering the music for the three Masses for the Feast of the Nativity is still beyond us; Volmar and I agreed on only one, and so it was the *Missa prima in galli cantu* we sang,[23] leaving at least a brief space for sleeping before Lauds and Prime. Festivities will come at midday, for three of the nearby families of my virgins

of penance and joyous expectation—was specially marked by the singing of the "O Antiphons." (Their name is derived from the "O" that initiates each text.) Most commonly there are seven of these antiphons; beginning on December 17th, the "Great O's" (*antiphonae majores*) were sung before and after the Magnificat at Vespers, and this practice continues today. Their language is characteristically that of Sapientia, who is that feminine aspect of the divine so long neglected and recently emerging in contemporary theological studies. Going back to the ancient choir books, we usually find eight "O Antiphons," beginning on the calendar at December 16th. The additional text is "O Virgin of virgins, how shall this be? For never was there one like you, nor will there ever be.—Daughters of Jerusalem, why do you look wondering at me? What you behold is a divine mystery." In addition, medieval monastic (as opposed to cathedral) calendars often list four additional "O Antiphons," probably used in special processions, and always beginning with that sense of wonder provided by the opening "O" followed by a noun of direct address. One of the rarest of these is "*O domina mundi*": "O Lady of the World, sprung of royal seed: from your womb Christ came forth as a bridegroom from his chamber; He lies in a manger who also rules the stars." (Trans. Burlin, *Advent*, p. 41.)

◼ 21. The Latin titles *domina* (Lady) and *abbatissa* (abbess) were nearly interchangeable in medieval women's monastic houses. Hildegard was herself

have insisted on sending their servants with portions of their feasts for our table. The joy of goose and duck, preserved quince, plus the first fruits of our own vineyards! We will warm the fowl in our ovens so the wonderful aroma fills the house, and the women will forgive all the fasting and boredom of salt herring and beer.

The ropes of green larch, and scents of pitch and resin from the boughs of pine fill our refectory and temporary chapel, and they are all nearly childishly delighted to prepare in this way for the feast. It is such a deep part of us, the need for green in the north, and no doubt in Rome and Jerusalem the birth is always attended in green. The martyr's palm I've seen in the precious manuscripts, their illuminations gilded and blessed with powdered lapis for the gown of the Virgin and gold for Her crown, the walls of the heavenly Jerusalem so studded with topaz, sapphire, and other jewels that the eye is dazzled with light. When the Christ rode into Jerusalem, the palms were fresh and green. Palms were used to sweep, to write texts upon, to crown the heads of those victorious in contests. How different from the dull, browning dry shards I have had as addressed both ways in letters, along with additional titles such as *mater* (mother) and *magistra* (teacher). (In English Benedictine houses the term "Dame" is still in use, and in this country the head of the Benedictine Abbey of Regina Laudis, Bethlehem, CT, is always addressed as Lady Abbess.)

▦ 22. Santiago de Compostela, in Galicia, now northwestern Spain, was so named because of the traditional belief that the body of the Apostle James (Sant'Iago), who was the first of the twelve disciples to be martyred, had been translated to that spot. The popularity of Santiago de Compostela as a destination for medieval pilgrimages from all over Europe was second only to that of Jerusalem and possibly to the tomb of the Apostles Peter and Paul in Rome.

▦ 23. Hildegard refers to Midnight Mass, "at the first cry of the cock," which celebrates the birth of the Word in eternity and of Christ in time. Only the Feast of the Nativity is assigned three Masses: a second is sung at dawn while a third or Day Mass celebrates the accomplished mystery.

gifts from pilgrims who stopped at Disibodenberg, breaking off sacred pieces to share the sense of their journeys!

For us, the light of Christ is eternal, but verdancy is seasonal. That which could be perpetually green is blighted by fire, drought, and frost. On this mountain, the light in October is magical, but in March the same light fails to stir us because there is no color to filter its angled rays. In October, we sense the light through the butter-yellow of delicate mulberry leaves, still hanging on and fluttering like perpetual candles, and bronze oaks whose leaves are saturated with royal garnet. And so the position of the sun is itself part of our ritual. The shortest day, the sharpest angle of the sun, absent of any real color, the hardest to bear in our bones, is made hopeful by the expectation already come with His birth. The solstice on the 21st is the point at which we start collecting the greens for Christmas Day.

But colorful journeys have been given to precious few women, and most of them we honor with the martyr's palm. Consider the passion of Ursula,[24] herself a long-awaited Christian child of King Deonotus in the British lands. Her *passio* tells us that ‡‡*while both her parents awaited with highest*

24. Just as the custom of embedding the holy relic of a martyr in the altar came to supplant the original practice of celebrating Mass upon the actual burial place, another common medieval development was the hagiography: From simple commemorative lists of saints and martyrs, narrative biographies, often rather formulaic, were elaborated. In the case of a martyr, the written account was called a *passio*. Such were used in sermons for the offices on the saints' feast days. The cult of St. Ursula & the 11,000 Virgins originated in Cologne, which was a part of Hildegard's diocese; it is most likely that two lengthy passions were known to her as she was composing her songs for St. Ursula. *Passio I* was written at the end of the 10th century by a Flemish monk for a convent of virgins in Cologne; *Passio II* was written before 1100 for nuns at a St. Ursula Foundation in Cologne, and it is from this that the Journal quotes. Both versions assign October 21st as the Feast Day of St. Ursula & the 11,000.

hope a male child who would be the successor to their earthly kingdom, God's provident mercy—which knows how to grant even more than is prayed for—gave them a female child. This daughter was endowed with a more than manly spirit, so that she might go before them to the inheritance of the heavenly kingdom, to which they would follow. In this way she could prepare for them many good things which would endure without end. Because she was destined one day to strangle the savage bear [that is, the Devil], following David's example, she received from her parents in baptism the prophetic name of Ursula [little bear]. This was done through the dispensation of God, for he names those whom he predestines.[25] ‡‡

Graced with radiant beauty and intelligence from the first, she was spoken for very early by the son of a foreign king who was politically strong, but unbaptized in the faith. When legates from the foreign prince formalized the proposal of marriage, King Deonotus brooded, weighing his beloved Ursula's devotion to Christ against the economic advantages of such a marriage for the two kingdoms, and for his daughter as well. The conflict was resolved by Ursula herself, when her vigil of prayer and fasting was rewarded with divine guidance assuring her perpetual virginity. A vision overtook Ursula with deep urgency, and she told her father that he should sign the agreement, that she would honor the marriage contract, but not until she had been allowed a three-year sea voyage to the holy places with virgin companions. Her pilgrimage granted and eleven ships fitted out, she was taunted and teased as she declared her yearning love for Christ, a passion that filled the very sails of the triremes and allowed her to abandon her espoused with such unearthly joy. Her single-mindedness and determination, her scorn for the things of this world, her fierce devotion to her vision, her firm insistence that it originated not in herself but in the Most High, ignited scorn and hatred from worldly men and a passionate devotion in her women companions.

There were holy men who honored them ❖ 25. Sheingorn & Thiébaux, trans., *Passion*, p. 16.

when Ursula set out like Abraham, leading an unlikely army of virgins across the sea as standard-bearers of Christ,[26] a truly royal contingent of holy women. Their voices raised, their music fanned the air and swelled to great volume as they progressed, even crossing the Alps, and, when they were struck down in the city of Cologne by the devilish Huns, pagan and eager to do the evil wishes of the Devil who hates music, the physical world convulsed in shock. Their crimson blood colored the water of the harbor, and the martyrdom of St. Ursula joined her forever to that of her beloved, her Lover of Light.

The precious bones of her band of women were buried in Cologne where they had been slaughtered like so many innocent lambs, and their relics are newly uncovered and sought after in our lifetime. But it is Ursula herself who inspires me, that woman so driven by the Holy Spirit to fulfill her journey that, to me, she is baptized "Columba" in her holy martyrdom: she is the chosen one, the one clothed in varieties of gold and sparkling jewels, whose sound is of the psalms and of the elemental rushing of waters.[27]

26. *Passio II* repeatedly refers to Ursula's women companions as an army, or military band of virgins; so Hildegard, in one of the narrative antiphons she composed, calls them the *vexillatae*, probably from the hymn "*Vexilla regis*" ("The Banners of the King") written in the 6th century by Venatus Fortunatus and sung at Vespers during the last two weeks of Lent. Hildegard's word *vexillata* seems to be a feminized combination of the Latin words *vexillum* (banner) and *vexillatio* (army fighting under one flag). The text of Hildegard's antiphon is in the Appendix.

27. Hildegard's little antiphons for St. Ursula & the 11,000 tell the story of their lives in a fairly straightforward narrative congruent with *Passios I* and *II*. Hildegard's hymn and sequence for the feast, however, are of an entirely different order. Their texts are visionary throughout; Ursula is depicted as a primordial female figure variously manifesting Ecclesia, Sapientia, the woman clothed in the sun from Apocalypse (Revelations) 12, and the Beloved of the Song of

The brilliance of her journey will surround my women here. Their pilgrimages will process from one stage of her illuminated vision to another. We will attend such a journey with many candles exulting, with evergreening boughs at Christmastide and dried martyrs' palms, burned and borne in ash on our foreheads during Lent. Processing to the Cross is the goal of Christmas, and we will be colored by boughs of green, candles of light singing with the echoing Dove. The long-awaited child in each of us will be born and blessed and nurtured in such vision.

Nothing seems to work as efficiently as it did in Disibodenberg, but I will not breathe a word of this to my women, they are so pulled down by their own complaints and discouragements. We are understandably still far from self-sufficiency in many things, but these grim winter months are the most constant reminder of how much harder is mere survival with the short hours of daylight and the relentless cold. Even the bell sounds of the Angelus were muffled this morning. The wet snow began in the evening, shortly after Compline, but tentatively, in localized, swirling gusts driven by a strong wind out of the northeast. My old portress

December 28, 1151
Feast of the Holy Innocents[28] and the Octave of Christmas[29]

Songs. The formal structure for Hildegard's hymn is a particularly dramatic one, in which several different voices alternate. It is the priests in this song who announce that, through her leadership and martyrdom, Ursula is rebaptized in her blood and thereby given the name of Columba (Dove); thus she is linked to the Holy Spirit. (Texts for these songs in Appendix.)

28. According to Matthew's Gospel (2:16–18), King Herod ordered the slaying of all children in Bethlehem under two years of age in an attempt to destroy the newborn Jesus. The feast appears on all medieval calendars for December 28th.

29. In the calendar, Octave, from the Latin word for "eighth day," denotes the Christian liturgical practice of continuing the celebration of

came to consult about putting down fireplace ashes for the last part of the climbing path, but it always seems worthwhile to wait out the storm before laying down ash. It can easily be covered in an hour's fall, and then the new fall freezes over it. The storm continued all night, and I was the first to wade into its depth before dawn.

I made my trip to the gate shortly before Lauds, as I do every morning at this season to watch the first light. The deep silence was not only due to the amount that blanketed the ground in soft waves like a sea floor; snow also lay in drifts on the winter-bare branches of deciduous trees, like soft clumps of sheep's wool bleached white by the pale winter sun. But no cloth that we weave is so starkly white as this snow; not sheep wool, goat hair, nor the mane of our palest horse. The white of our wimples and veils looks soiled and dark by comparison.

Timbers for our cloister church, some half-hoisted into place, others laid out on the ground like the pieces of a remarkable puzzle, began to emerge. The bowl of sky behind was first yellow as a lemon, with those ink-black, squared-off silhouettes vaulting up and against it. One softer pink corner appeared in the extreme lower right stretch of horizon; the yellow paled further as the real rose of dawn emerged, giving the cut and shaped timbers both color and dimension. With my hands snug in new knitted gauntlets and each tucked into the other's sleeve, I stayed warm enough to watch both cut timbers and live rooted trees emerge and take on full form in first light. Timbers and trees both speak for the solidity that will mark our cloister church. They assure me that—unlike the early fortunes of Disibodenberg, of communities that come and go, appear and fail— ours will remain.[30] Our community will stabilize, major feasts for a full week, ending on the eighth day after the feast itself. During the Middle Ages, this practice applied not only to such large, movable feasts as the Nativity, Easter, and Pentecost; it was extended as well to fixed feasts of important saints such as the Apostles, Agnes, and the Virgin Mary.

30. According to chronicles, the early history of Disibodenberg was relatively unstable, and,

and we will ultimately have agreement about the architectural expression of our spirit.

It has not been easy, the planning of the cloister church. Oh, the name, the translation of the relics,[31] the finding of a stone suitable in size and color in which to house the sacred bones, these were relatively simple matters, determined by custom and by reliable witnesses to the sacred life of Rupert, his early mission and history on this mountainside, now our sacred inheritance.[32] He is honored in our coming, and his bones are now in our sacred trust. Much more complex are decisions about the height of our church, the nature of its glass: Should it be of dazzling color—the heavenly Jerusalem's jeweled walls expressed as they are in the Cluniac houses, as urged by Odo[33]—or is it as Br. Bernard so vehemently insists,

between 1098 and 1105, the monks had abandoned it. (Schmitt, *American Benedictine Review*, p. 174.)

31. "Translation" or the practice of moving one or more sacred bones of a saint from the original burial place to its burial in an altar was honored liturgically with the Mass for the Dedication of a Church. Relics could also be housed in specially designed shrines and reliquaries. If the saint so honored was considered important enough, a new liturgical feast might be created—in addition to the *die natalis* (marking the date of the person's death, literally the day of their birth into heaven), the date marking the actual translation might also be added to the liturgical calendar.

32. Hildegard founded her convent on the site of a ruined church, monastery, and tomb that had been built through the generosity of the mother of a holy German nobleman named Rupert. Hildegard did a great deal to revive, if not create reverence for St. Rupert, whose youthful pilgrimage, piety, and death made him an inspiring subject for one of the abbess's artfully constructed sequences, to be sung for Mass on his feast. Her cloister church was dedicated, on May 1, 1152, to SS. Philip, Martin, and James, and to the Virgin Mother of God. (Newman, *Symphonia*, p. 295.)

33. Frankish Benedictine monk (eventually canonized as St. Odo), he became abbot of Cluny (Burgundy) in 927 and is credited with building the influence of that

that the open space of the Cistercian houses, with their clear glass, the honest and simple proportions themselves, carry the Divine Office more directly to the Most High? I still tend towards color, the warmth and passion of representation and color. I believe that, as my women and I enter into liturgical time, through the contemplative act of singing, we can also focus and meditate upon representations of exemplary lives painted on the ceiling or the walls that will mirror our sounds in a spectrum of color.[34]

Most of all I hope to have the whole journey of St. Ursula and her virgins spread around us like the sides of the world—a map of her journey, a record of her travels, colored in the finest paints and powders we can find and afford. For most of my women, the journey will be an inner one entirely, a point of initiation ritualized in a Ceremony of Consecration, in which their veiling and clothing is the outer sign of ever-deepening vows; later, moments of illumination, doses of learning and accomplishment, texts understood and inscribed in their hearts and minds, songs of praise spun out of their mouths like feathery, winged September seeds. Very few will pass beyond these walls before they die, but they must have an urgent sense of movement and direction.

To most of this I will myself attend, with Volmar's support and still greater experience in matters of learning. I can read

house to the extent that many other Benedictine houses in Italy and France modeled themselves upon the Cluniac reforms. Cluny achieved its greatest influence in the 11th and 12th centuries, at which time its economic and artistic achievement was most splendid.

▨ 34. Stave churches in Scandinavia remain as examples of the earlier Romanesque practice of painting highly colored narrative scenes and didactic arrangements of mythological, Biblical, and saintly figures on the wooden walls and/or ceilings in churches long since rebuilt or destroyed by fires and wars. Alternatively, paintings were sometimes made directly on the masonry walls of Romanesque churches, but the vast majority of these were "modernized"— replaced by very different structures with quantities of stained glass windows and Gothic openwork during the High Middle Ages and into the Renaissance.

to them, focus their minds through texts, sung and spoken, through attention to the smallest detail of liturgy and of the quality of their communal life. There is also the beauty of paint and color as they find themselves fairly embedded in a matrix of meaning.

We argue constantly about the outside shape and style of the church. No one apparently believes that I—a mere woman, frail and untaught—have seen enough of the architectural jewels of the world to understand what we need.

 I am so little interested in His humanity that the voguish wave for depicting His tender birth and infancy repels me.[36] The Cistercians write whole treatises on these subjects, are moved to circulate them among their ever-proliferating houses, as a salve to all of us,

January 6, 1152
Feast of the Epiphany[35]

warm ointment, a moist balm for our consciences. How little I need reminding about the pathetic nature of being human. What glory in circulating stories of His humble birth, His sharing a stall with smelly animals, His birthing in straw, Her swollen discomfort in searching out a place of respite, teetering hugely on a clumsy, plodding ass, poor beast of burden? Surely this is not to elevate or soothe the masses of humanity living just that

35. Greek word meaning "manifestation," this feast was introduced in the West from the Eastern Church in the 4th century. It celebrates the manifestation of Christ to the Gentiles, through the persons of the Magi. Until modern times, Epiphany had both an Octave and a Vigil, and, in Catholic Spanish-speaking countries, it remains more important than the Feast of the Nativity.

36. All of Hildegard's writings substantiate the fact that she was going against the growing theological concern and writings about the humanity of Jesus—the details of His human birth and infancy, as well as those of His suffering. Similarly, Hildegard's extensive portrayals of the Virgin present Her not at all as the human mother of Jesus, but in Her numinous or divine aspect, as with Sapientia, Ecclesia, and the female Virtues of her *Ordo virtutum*.

way, braying with asses, who swarm the countryside, drag themselves into our parish and monastic churches, looking to us for signs of something better than they can know, they with their rough hands and dirty feet. Why feed the laity with more stories about suffering humanity?

And what more do I need to know of humanity, with our fallen selves in painful evidence everywhere? Behold the humanity of the clergy, the worldly clerics and priests so easily bought and sold as they run after temporal as well as ecclesiastical power. Such comfort to know that He was not only Christ the King, but now the poor human Jesus: So the clergy are comforted in their human laxity and irresponsibility, and misguided as to their fitness for elevation in office.

Let Him remain in His majesty, enthroned with His mother suspended on a pillar of light, the ever-turning crest of the fountain! The more I can explain and classify the known elements, the huge families of plants and trees, minerals, animals, and color-filled wonders of this world, all the more inspired I am to sing of its secrets: the mystery of grace, the grandeur of His saving, the wonders of Ecclesia's healing, light-giving love, and the terrifying powers of darkness—for all of these are much larger than simple humanity.

The Dragon's dark powers are wily and concentrated,[37] and I seem to be dealing with them constantly. The most beautifully embodied souls are his prey, and with such trophies would he decorate his world. His desire for them is endless, and his potency undiluted by doubts, care, reason, or love. Little enough does he care about humanity, save to vie with the glory of God, and that single-mindedness gives him great persuasive power. He hates music, opposes it everywhere for its beauty and true power in praise of the divine mysteries he

🔲 37. For Hildegard, the Devil is a powerful reality. She often refers to him with the Latin word *draco* (Dragon), in a form reminiscent of that beast in the Book of the Apocalypse. She may also refer to him as the Evil One, the Tempter, or *Diabolus*; or—always with more subtlety and respect—as Lucifer, who, before his banishment, tried to be a lamp, rather than a mirror for God.

would unravel and drown like wet kittens. I could never oppose him nor persist in ferreting him out of helpless bodies, if I thought we were merely so much fallen humanity.

Constantly, recurrently, and with greatest anguish have I experienced my own powerlessness in the face of suffering. Entire days, Octaves, and Seasons have found me prostrate on my bed and wracked with pain, feverish with unrealized plans for my women, never-ending pressure behind my eyes, and knowing only that the ears of authority are deaf to my pleas. Tell me about fallen humanity, and you drown me in its helpless waves of misery! Of what possible use to tell me drivel about suffering humanity! For I have rolled plentifully in my own; I've witnessed the smelly, helpless birthing and slow, anguished dying of the healthy as well as the sick: arbitrary and humanly senseless.

Only God's grace has saved me. Do not remind me, then, of anyone's suffering! Tell me of the sparks of divinity, tell me stories of the uplifting by God's green finger of the most despised of us all. Tell me of the glory of an Ursula who saw and followed an impossible vision, attracting untold thousands of frail women into the gleaming mystery of her divine beauty. Tell me of saints whose human powers were so uneven, humours so unbalanced,[38] yet who shimmered in their triumphs over powers of darkness.

38. Typical medicophysical beliefs in the 12th century, originating in Greek scientific thought, linked physiology and cosmology through complex quaternities of four elements, four qualities (hot, cold, moist, and dry) and four humours or temperaments (choleric, sanguine, phlegmatic, and melancholic). As in the rest of her thinking, Hildegard's formulation of these ideas is heterodox rather than formulaic. According to her descriptions, each of the four humours interact with other physical and emotional characteristics, affecting a person's sexual and reproductive capacities, among other things. Basically, there is a particular hierarchical balance of humours, qualities, and elements that is desirable. Whenever this optimal condition is upset either constitutionally or temporarily, illness results. If the imbalance is severe and constitutional (as is the case with Hildegard herself), only God's grace can make it right.

We all thirst so after beauty, after openings into the vault of heaven, after sights and sounds capable of transcending the all-too-human sizes and shapes we assume, the well-defined and measured restrictions on what is possibly human.

Our simple limitations impress me not at all. They collapse the vault of heaven and dry up the dripping red rose of divine promise.

And so I go into battle with the stupidity of those men who still will not grant that we have earned our right to hold and manage all the lands of our well-dowered women.

Do you think that the winning of all I have won has a shred to do with my humanity? No; what inspires people to listen at all are the divine sparks, the prophetic power of the mysteries I have sung and described, beauties so clear to my inner senses that they color in dazzling green and gold the tendril and branch of every vine and tree shrouding the hills between the rivers Nahe and Rhine.

Volmar thinks we're ready this year and suggests I think about receiving public penitents for the period of Lent.[40] Directing them to bed down with the sheep is surely best for all, since they can neither bathe nor shoe their feet during this interval. Some warmth will keep them there, and their cries of separation, longing for missed family and loved ones, will blend into the bleating of sheep and nickering of goats. If they will truly honor their fasting and keep from sucking the full udders and warm teats of those ewes yet to lamb, they can share the clean straw, hear ani-

January 18, 1152

Feast of St. Prisca, Martyr[39]

39. The St. Prisca known to Hildegard was a Roman martyr whose relics were translated to the Roman church named for her during the 4th century. Her feast day was celebrated on January 18th throughout the Western Church in medieval times, and she was popularly portrayed between the two lions who apparently had refused to attack her.

40. Imposition of public penance (as well as private, for less serious and social sins) on Ash

mals converse while keeping silence, yet know some comfort.

Our Lenten cloth grows larger and larger on the loom; I pray that it will be ready for the Lenten Season. Suspended in front of the sanctuary, and richly purple, it will not only symbolize being cut off from the sight of the altar in this long time of penance, it will also serve to insulate us against the bitter northeast winds that come most nights with Compline. If only the light would last a little longer, the sisters could return to the work for a bit after the evening office without breaking the Great Silence.[41] Perhaps we need to place the loom inside the chapter house where western exposure will capture the lengthening light between Vespers and Compline. Sister Birgitte has devised coverings for the hands, knitted for each palm, ramifying for digits, but leaving all the fingertips exposed to allow the sensitive threading of warp and weft.

Meanwhile, this winter week has been unbearable for all of us. I suffer silently, but bitter cold sits

Wednesday was a common practice in the medieval Church; its strictures were kept until Holy Thursday, when the solemn rite of reconciliation was enacted. In addition to being banished from the Church for the period, public penitents usually spent the period of Lent doing charitable acts of manual labor. Often their voluntary confinement was at a monastery, where they slept on the ground and were required to remain barefoot and unwashed (Weiser, *Christian Feasts*, p. 175).

41. Period of absolute silence strictly maintained in all religious communities. This time is intended for communication with God only, and can take the form of silent prayer, contemplation, reading, writing, or liturgical participation in the Office or Mass. Most commonly the Great Silence is designated as extending each day from the end of Compline through the end of Lauds or Mass the following morning. Matins, the night Office and most deeply contemplative of the eight, thus falls within the given period. No one in the religious community is allowed to speak to another during the length of the Great Silence. (The use of sign language is not uncommon when the need for communication is urgent.)

in my joints, and sharp daggers of ice assault my entire spine. Knitting woolen undergarments becomes more valued in this house than singing psalms, and lay sisters serve the choir nuns with their skilled hands. Some of the turnips and rutabagas have frozen in the root cellar and turn to mush in the soup. Sr. Adelgundis continues to weaken herself by stealthily avoiding food for the twelfth day. I will speak with her once more.

Other things progress. I have examined three more women recommended from our town of Bingen, bringing them up the steep mountain by sledge through the snow. They are indeed steeped in the wisdom of herbs and medicinals; I am sure they can be relied upon to make the first gathering in late March. By that time, I need to begin cataloging these precious substances, assigning their places in the great design of healing, their respective qualities and curative powers.[42] For some, the season of safe gathering is so short; pokeweed, for example, comes so quickly in the spring and as quickly becomes toxic—producing deadly hallucinations—so there needs to be a kind of calendar as part of the catalog. Perhaps we also need a map, no matter how crudely drawn, figured by these wise old women, drawn by one of my lettered women—the infirmarian maybe—so that locations of vital medicines become commonly known to the lay sisters. Even Clothild, blind for six years now, can be taught to recognize the square stems of the mint family by touch, further differentiating by smell whether it is pennyroyal, spearmint, nepeta, or our carefully tended bed of patchouli, its seeds brought back as a gift from the Jerusalem War, its oil so thick and precious, to be saved for our sacramental anointing of throats and brows.

How like the miracle of God's usage of us, this naming and calling into being of plants! Volmar warns that I am criticized for spending so much time on the planning of our crops, for my attention to the details of healing and medicinals, and for my desire to catalog

42. Hildegard was working on her medicophysical treatises, known to us as the *Physica* and the *Causae et curae*.

what is available to us on this mountain for healing the sick. Without such attention, plants grow wild in the meadows, on the slopes and stream banks, but they live only by chance in a chaos of potential. They require naming, calling into being, description, use, and—in some cases—careful cultivation and fertilization in order to enhance their size, vitality, and curative powers. Such is the power of naming, baptism, the recognition of vocation, the promise of obedience. How I wish that each of my women, in their clothing and consecration, could formally take on a new name for this new life.[43]

St. Agnes[44] is the best exemplar for our meditation. Let them consider what the good Bishop St. Ambrose said about her. In the 2nd Lesson of her Matins office, he says, "But how shall I set forth the glory of her whose very name is an utterance of praise? It seems to me that this being, holy beyond her years, and strong beyond human nature, received the name of Agnes, not as an earthly designation,

43. The custom of taking a new name "in religion" was not yet the practice for Benedictine nuns in Hildegard's time; nevertheless, it is clear from the contemporary monastic texts that the issue was already important, with its roots in the Old Testament power of naming.

44. Agnes, most highly honored virgin martyr in the primitive Church, was venerated in Rome from the 4th century. She was extolled in hymns and texts by all the outstanding writers, such as Augustine, Ambrose, and Prudentius, and liturgical texts for her feast became prototypes for those of many other women saints as they were added to the Roman Martyrology and calendar. The outstanding features of her life, according to biographies written in the 5th century, are the fact that she refused marriage, consecrated her virginity to God, and was martyred by stabbing in the throat (a common Roman method of execution). All texts in her honor agree on her voluntary admission of faith at a historical time of imperial edicts against Christianity, her extreme youth (either twelve or thirteen) at the time of martyrdom, and her heroism under torture. Iconographically, she is usually pictured with a lamb, since her name is a variant of the Latin *agnus* (lamb) which links her directly to Christ, who is the *Agnus dei* (Lamb of God).

but as a revelation from God of what she was to be." So I believe it is with St. Ursula. Her sacred life, which I have read again and again, tells us the significance of her naming—the fierce little she-bear, who, like David, God intended to fight the giant. The very climax of my hymn for her bears witness to this sacred power of naming, and so I have the priests—those who have official ordination—say to her women:

> *"O Most excellent flock,*
> *This virgin who on earth is called Ursula*
> *Is named in highest heaven Columba...."* [45]

She is consecrated in the name of the Holy Spirit, just as Agnes has received the name of the Christ, the Lamb, the one chosen of God.

Let my women listen carefully as they sing the canticles for the lessons of the 3rd Nocturn of Matins on Agnes's feast, "and thou shalt be called by a new name, which the mouth of the Lord shall name. And thou shalt be a crown of glory in the hand of the Lord, and a royal diadem in the hand of thy God.... Thou shalt no more be called Forsaken, and thy land shall no more be called Desolate: but thou shalt be called My pleasure in her, and thy land inhabited." [46] Let them understand the exceptional possibilities of being called into a vocation whose very nature is that of virginal fecundity.

To be a lily of the field is enough. To be a lily whose color is exceptional

45. Lines from Hildegard's hymn *"Cum vox sanguinis"* (When the voice of the blood of Ursula), translated in full in Appendix.

46. From the monastic office of Matins in the Common of Virgins; the latter, which was being codified precisely during Hildegard's lifetime, contains all of the melodies and sung texts used for the feasts of virgins of the Church, except for those few that are proper to the particular saint and written exclusively for her. In a similar way, there developed a Common of Apostles, a Common of Bishops, and so on for each category of those honored, thus providing a basic group of songs to be learned as the number of saints proliferated during the period.

in the light that God casts upon it, to be fertilized and watered, encouraged to grow, to provide beauty and even shade and support in some cases, is more. But to be transformed and renamed in that calling is the greatest grace, and is to grow into the limbs of the Tree of Life.[47]

Talking with Volmar would be a comfort. His

January 20, 1152

Feast of St. Agnes, Virgin and Martyr

way of listening would perhaps allow even more of the meaning to come out and might also make the experience less frightening. The first one started on the night of the Vigil for the Feast of Epiphany, which must be more than two weeks ago now. The dreams seem to begin shortly before I hear the waking bells for Matins, and, once we have completed the office, I promptly fall back into the same murky place and dream a variation on the same dream that preceded Matins.[48]

Several times the frightening characters in the dreams have hovered around

47. Hildegard's insistence on conflating tree and body imagery has a long history in mystical and liturgical Christianity: it is a joining together of Christ's discourse after the Last Supper (according to John 15:1–17) and the Pauline image of the Body of Christ (Ephesians 2:13–16 and 3:4–6). In Hildegard, the limbs of Christ are figured in the Tree of Life in the Garden of Paradise, identified with the Rood (Tree) upon which Christ was crucified, and seen in the proud female Tree of Wisdom (Ecclesiasticus 1:20–25 and 24:12–21). The tree imagery appears characteristically in Hildegard's lyrical songs for women, where, for example, the Virgin is described as having the birds of heaven nest in Her and is addressed directly as "O viridissima virga" (O greenest branch). This strong emphasis on "treeness" and "greenness" also has deep roots in Hildegard's Teutonic heritage, which includes the pre-Christian reverence for the Sacred Oak that Boniface (the "Apostle of Germany") destroyed in the 8th century, and the World Tree on which the Norse god Odin was sacrificed for knowledge of the runes.

48. According to the Rule of St. Benedict, the singing of the Divine Office at night (Matins) differs from winter

my head during Matins, so much so that I can feel their hissing breath in my ear during all three of the Nocturns. Always so much is demanded of me: I am somehow responsible for the impending deaths and the debilitating illnesses of hundreds of people, all of them relatively unknown to me. It is not clear in what way I am responsible—only that I am responsible and there is something I must do.

Sometimes the hordes of people who are sick don't even speak a language I understand. At least once upon waking I thought they might be Saracens, Greeks, infidels from the Holy Land, or Albigensians from the south of France, people whose souls cry out for conversion, whose language cannot reach my ears, who do not know the cadences of Latin because they are unbaptized.

The restlessness these dreams have caused me is remarkable considering how little of substance actually transpires in them, how little I understand or even remember what has happened in those minutes—or is it hours?—when they invade my sleep. And where is it happening exactly? Most of all, I wonder about the source of such dreams.

Surely they are not in the same category as my visions, for those come to me when my eyes are open, through my inner senses,

to summer: "During winter—from November first until Easter—the brothers [sic] shall rise at the eighth hour of the night [2 A.M.] as is reasonable; thus having rested a bit more than half the night, they will be refreshed. Any time left over ought to be used by the brothers to practice psalms or for reading. From Easter until November first the hour for Matins should be arranged so that, after a very short break for going to the toilet, Lauds, which ought to be said at daybreak, may follow immediately." (Trans. Meisel & del Mastro, *The Rule of St. Benedict*, New York, 1975 [hereinafter *RB*], p. 61.) In addition, the practice was modified from community to community. In general, a return to sleep, contemplation, prayer, or reading was usual in winter when nights were so much longer. In summer, Matins would be sung later, followed immediately by Lauds, thereby using the long daylight hours to best advantage for work periods.

in the clear light of day, but lit from above, in the Shadow of the Living Light. These dreams that are plaguing me come only when I am deeply, nearly deathly, asleep, in a sleep that is both deeper and more troubled than is normal for me. And how do they prophesy? Not in the sense of telling future events, for we do not normally understand the gift or act of prophecy in that way. When Daniel was able to explain the dreams of Nebuchadnezzar, the signs and gestures that were presented had meanings connected to the divine mysteries, even though the dreamer himself was an infidel. And of the other Old Testament prophets, their role was never to predict, but to interpret. Just so, in my visions, the Voice of Wisdom explains the significance of particular colors and figures, the lessons and meanings condensed into gestures, actions, and even tableaux that unfold to me in the Shadow of the Living Light.[49]

These dreams are different: unclear and confusing, without any interpreting voice, they are never direct with me. What is their relationship to me? Is it possible they could be of the Devil? Of course this is what I fear most and what has pre-

49. As an old woman, Hildegard described very clearly the two different ways in which her visions presented themselves to her, in a letter to Guibert of Gembloux. (The letter caused Guibert to leave everything he was doing and become her secretary for the last few years of her life, following the death of Volmar.) In the letter, Hildegard observes that "The brightness I see is not spatial, yet it is far, far more lucent than a cloud that envelops the sun. I cannot contemplate height or length or breadth in it; and I call it 'the shadow of the living brightness.' And as sun, moon and stars appear [mirrored] in water, so Scriptures, discourses, virtues, and some works of men take form for me and are reflected radiant in this brightness.... And in that same brightness I sometimes, not often, see another light, which I call 'the living light'; when and how I see it, I cannot express; and for the time I do see it, all sadness and all anguish is taken from me, so that then I have the air of an innocent young girl and not of a little old woman." (Trans. Dronke, *Women Writers of the Middle Ages*, Cambridge, 1984 [hereinafter *WWMA*], p. 168.)

vented me from speaking about them as yet to Volmar, a poor decision on my part. Is the old Dragon at it again, and just how is he trying to get at me this time? And what, specifically, could I have done that evoked him, if it is he in the guise of my recent bouts of dreaming?

The last time I felt he was sniffing me out—for he is closely connected to the sense of smell, almost "an olfactory presence," you might say (I feel I can smell him and he in turn is sniffing me out)—I protected myself with the power of chanted prayer and words. He is repelled by our singing the Divine Office, and we in our singing expressly exclude, almost preclude his being, through the act of praising God with our voices.[50]

That was the time when Engwis had the issue of blood. She was hemorrhaging so that it left her whole face and body skin the color of lead. The rhythms in her wrists were faint but racing, and we all feared she could be without life if the loss of blood continued even a day or two longer. I knew there was a connection between Christ's blood and her issuance of blood. Only the King Himself could in His mercy staunch and heal what was already beyond human bodily endurance. We had already applied poultices, bindings, warmth and cold, herbs specific and general, tried elevation of the lower

50. Hildegard wrote down her lifelong and passionate beliefs about music during the last year of her life in a letter to the prelates of Mainz. Deprived by interdict of the daily singing of the Divine Office, she produced a lengthy, reasoned argument for what amounts to a theology of music in which all sacred music—instrumental as well as vocal—functions as the bridge for humanity to life before the Fall. She claims that the *spiraculo* (God's breath that created the first human life [Genesis 2:7]) is to be used to sing the praises of God, either with the sound of voices or with instruments, as we are reminded again and again in Psalm 150; and that the Devil, as soon as he heard humankind singing through the inspiration of God, began to oppose it, which he has done consistently ever since. Hildegard's beliefs also informed her decision, in her sung morality play *Ordo virtutum*, to have the Devil be the one character without any music to sing.

body and night-long vigils of prayer by the professed choir nuns in rotation. There was a need to formalize the prayer—to instrumental-ize it—to make it nearly a sacrament of blood, equating the blood that poured out of the lance-pierced side with the blood that gushed from the womb of this simple woman who had desperately sought our help. If a liturgical act was required to embody the prayer, there was none; in that faith, thus I spoke: ‡‡*In the blood of Adam death arose; in the blood of Christ death was restrained. In that same blood of Christ I command you, blood, to cease your flowing.*[51] ‡‡ It was clear enough to me then that I must protect myself from the Devil in this act, that he was lurking, and that my calling forth the blood of Christ for this simple woman could open me to him. By the grace of God, Engwis did recover, and the Devil was put down again.

Perhaps now he is opening up his old quarrel with me. Is it another guise of the heavily populated dream that disturbs and frightens me? There are some of his characteristics I recognize; for example, wherever he appears, he threatens my identity. He threatens my authority to act, to speak, to heal, to sing. My role becomes obscure, my responsibilities vague but overwhelming. There is nothing I am actually empowered to do; only everywhere there is the felt accusation that, had I been able to understand those undecipherable words and gestures, I might have prevented needless suffering in scores of people.

Is this pride? That in itself is enough to evoke the Devil.

Then again, the meaning could be so much simpler, so much more benign. The dreams could be speaking to me, and through me to my women, of the need to understand more about the nature of responsibility. Perhaps they are simply telling me I must use the time in refectory or in chapter to talk about responsibility. Enough, I will talk with Volmar, my trusted *magister*.

51. Translation of Hildegard's "healing charm" from the MS Vienna Nationalbibliothek, Cod. 1016, by Barbara Newman, *Sister of Wisdom*, Berkeley, 1987, p. 33.

The relationship between women and blood is ongoing,

February 2, 1152
Sexagesima Sunday[52] and Purification of the Virgin Mary[53]

and it is crucial for me to understand it, whether in an ancient ritualized form as with the Mother of Christ in Her purification, or the hemorrhaging that threatened the life of Engwis and could only be stanched in its relation to the blood of Christ. In the case of my Ursula, her passion is so womanly and zealous, her blood so heated in her desire for consummation, that its shedding at her martyrdom becomes a sign of her royalty, precious in the sight and service of God. Her womanly blood, shed out of love for Christ, endows her with a kind of divine and immortal protection against evil. The special antiphon I have done for her to be sung at the office canticle will make that clear:

> *O royal redness of blood,*
> *You flowed down from a high place*
> *Which divinity has touched;*
> *You are the flower that winter never damaged*
> *With the freezing blast of the Serpent.*[54]

For me, at this age, the bleeding is nearly finished: the unpleasant smells and chafing, the endless soiling and washing of cloths, the bloating of breasts and swelling of ankles. Nevertheless, compared with the pains I have endured in my bones and joints, the awful sensitivity behind my eyes to certain light—my own monthly cycles have never been severe enough to distract me from liturgical cycles, their duties and offices.

52. Sexagesima (sixtieth), its date movable (dependent on the date of Easter in the given year), refers to the Sunday that falls two weeks before the beginning of Lent, or approximately sixty days before Easter. This name appears as early as the 6th century.

53. In medieval times the Purification, a fixed feast falling on February 2nd, was considered one

For three of my women, the monthly bleeding is agony. I sometimes hear them sounding like desperate, wild she-cats in the night, their moans and gasps muffled and the more penetrating for all that effort at concealment. The particular configuration of planets at each one's birth I could guess but would not ask. They have died to the world, but what they suffer in their bodies is real enough, Holy Mother of God. I have given them each meditations on things of holy beauty as well as strenuous responsibilities out-of-doors to exercise them physically. They function well in choir; two of them are perhaps even more quick of mind than most, but some bodily fixation prevents the physical problem from being transformed through their immortal souls. In Christ we are neither male nor female, I remind them; the soul is the bride of Christ, I repeat. But the painful disjuncture persists, and, as stern as I am with all three of them, my reasoning heart knows that their suffering is real—though I

of the Marian feasts; its name derived from the ritual practice under Jewish law that took place forty days after childbirth. Since 1960, the Roman Church counts it as a feast of the Lord, having renamed it the Presentation of Christ in the Temple. Liturgically, the Purification celebrates the events recounted in the Gospel of St. Luke (2:31–39) that culminate in the Song of Simeon, inspired by the Holy Spirit; hence, the name Candlemas in England and Candelaria in Spanish-speaking countries, since the action on that day symbolically proclaims through a procession of lighted candles Simeon's words that Jesus was the Christ, "a light to lighten the Gentiles, and the glory of thy people Israel." This feast marks the end of the Christmas-Epiphany cycle.

▨ 54. In the two manuscripts we have for Hildegard's liturgical songs (Dendermonde, Klosterbibliothek, Cod. 9, ca. 1175, and Riesenkodex, Hessische Landesbibliothek, Hs 2, compiled within the decade following her death), the intensely lyrical antiphon quoted above is set off singly from the eight additional antiphons for St. Ursula and the 11,000. The latter are designated for use at the office of Lauds, undoubtedly to be used at Vespers as well, and present a more straightforward, consecutive narrative of the legend.

can increase my demands on their performance in any area of our monastic life and they will fulfill it to the letter. Something yet unknown to me is required for healing such rifts. It is of course grace, which is divine, over which I have no control, which can only be prayed for; but, if it should come, it must also have a way of taking root in their physical natures.

In the meantime, herbs and some minerals are a temporary and only partial solution, for while they ease the monthly pains and holding of fluid, the sounds I hear are not only those of suffering but of a longing in the world that I fully expected would recede—at least in the case of Sr. Birgitte—with her Ceremony of Consecration. Her lineage is perhaps the best of any of my women, but her humour is melancholic, and it would not be prudent for me to treat her condition as either disobedience or weakness. One of my lay sisters, Helge, a corporeal behemoth but wise and generous in her knowledge of healing, serves in the dispensary now with skilled hands and tells me of certain techniques of breathing. She claims that they balance and join these warring factions of body and soul, and I defer to her judgment in this case. Tomorrow I will assign Sr. Birgitte to duties in the dispensary.

I feel lonely in these matters.

 The Purification is behind us, the Season of Lent begins in exactly one week, and thoughts about losing Rikkarda continue to distract me. Let her be gone, I keep thinking, but my constant prayers ask that she remain in community with us always. Letters to her mother the marchioness go unanswered, and the peremptory tone in the recent letter from my heretofore supporter Henry,

February 5, 1152
Feast of St. Agatha,
Virgin and Martyr[55]

55. Agatha, martyred at Catania, in Sicily, was venerated from the 5th century as patron saint of that city. She is also patron saint for bell-founders and against fires, is pictured with bells, loaves, or her breasts on a platter, all derived from the physical tortures she suffered. According

archbishop of Mainz, suggests what I know far better than he: Although she is still young, her leadership skills set her apart from the rest, shine in her like Venus in the blackening, yellow-streaked dusk of winter skies. But prioress here—is that not sufficient to hold her?

Surely she knows how necessary she has been to our arrival here. Would the prelates of Mainz ever have supported me, finally facilitated our move from Disibodenberg without the support and generosity of her mother the marchioness? Was the Tempter himself already whispering in her ear about higher placement when, caught in the lashing whirlwind of our first year here, I looked into steady gray eyes within the rare planes of her forehead-to-cheekbones, sensed her rapt inner attention, and read there a deeply contemplative state? Was it never love that I felt from the moisture of her sweet breath as we discussed the endless details of the move, nor compassion from her long-fingered hands that I trusted to turn me on my bed at Disibodenberg? For months, as Abbot Kuno continued to oppose our move, the pain in my body seemed to radiate from my core to every curve and surface to such a degree that the sensation of my own much-diminished weight contacting the hard pallet beneath me was like the relentless bruising of blunt stones. That was the longest bout of illness so far, when the alternate shuddering and burning of my frame—more, of my very guts—parched my throat until it became a papery husk that rattled, peeling my lips in such dry shreds that the wetness of my bleeding mouth surprised me for its moisture and salt.

She was there as well through earlier bouts, before I began writing the *Scivias*. Even then, I knew what I wanted to say, what the visions were telling

to legend, Agatha dedicated her virginity to Christ, rejecting a certain Quintinian, who then persecuted her as a Christian. She was subjected to brutal tortures (including that of fire) that centered on her sexuality. Finally, her breasts were cut off, and although she enjoyed a miraculous healing through a vision of St. Peter, she eventually died in prison. Like Agnes, her name has for nearly 1500 years occurred in the canon of the Roman Mass.

me and had been telling me for so long. Still, silence seemed the only possibility in those days, while all the time the forms and pictures emerged in my wracked self at accelerating intervals, insinuating themselves from a shadowy flicker into light more sparkling than the noonday sun on the Rhine in July, the sun so brilliant that I've watched it suddenly tear and then lift away huge canopies of fog hanging late in the valley. When Rikkarda listened and understood, when Abbot Kuno finally accepted my vision, when Volmar listened and insisted on writing down what I told him, then the relentless pain would lift and be burnt away like that fog, would lift right out of my body, accompanied by the Voice of Wisdom, melodious, arching in modulations that build and play upon one another like music.

Today, the hymn that arose in me seemed threaded together as it came, in a way that I have not heard before. The music did not repeat with each new section of the words as hymns so often do; nor did I hear the rhythmic alternation of textures that comes when antiphonal voices sing in turn, the way we sing our psalms for the offices each day. And it does not emerge the way music happens when a particular antiphon sets off a familiar psalm, clarifying its meaning by juxtaposition, as though lifting the sapphire from its clasp of heavy gold to a more open filigreed winding, a tracery of sheen that plumbs its depths and alters its color.

The shaping of this hymn is more subtle; it has its varieties, but is threaded together from start to the end. Like a string of gold, one continuous voice seemed to shimmer beneath the sounds like a drone that moves but rarely from its resting place. It somehow gives voice to sound that was always there, dreaming its way through the fabric of the melody, allowing that main melody to loop and swirl to farther reaches the way an endless and flexible tether connects the plump ram to the roaming mountain ewes, serving them well. As they climb higher and higher, surefooted in the powdery-soiled crags, they nuzzle delicate strawberries in openings of meadows, surprising the nesting ovenbird higher yet to where hyssops and heathers are gray like the lichened rocks they adorn, but richer for the mineraled soil they spring from. The ewes are pulled on towards the sun by a thinner, rarer air closer to the ether that touches the firmament itself. And perhaps it is the smell of the stud ram, the sheer fragrance of the horned stolidity of him that acts like the invisible tether, both connecting and freeing, and ultimately drawing them back.

But I have gone very far afield in trying to understand the newness of the way this music moves.[56] This time I have gone so far I have nearly succeeded in forgetting about Rikkarda.

February 12, 1152
Ash Wednesday

 We are building the Heavenly Jerusalem out of sound and light, carving out the two choirs of the cloister church for our antiphonal singing. In doing this, we become

56. Hildegard did not speak metaphorically when she referred to her music as a *canticum novum* (a new song or chant), and it is only within the last decade that musicologists have begun to understand its originality. During her lifetime, Hildegard had a remarkable consciousness that the monody she produced was radically different from the great body of chant she inherited and sang day and night. In the latter, fairly rigid (often formulaic) conventions governed the structure of hymn, sequence, and responsory, for example. Hildegard wrote all of her own texts, and they adhered to none of the traditional rules of prosody or rhyme. Her melodies—their unusually wide range, word-painting, inspired leaps, and absolute refusal to abide by the rules of any one of the eight Church modes—are equally nontraditional. What Hildegard was "discovering" and what she describes above about her hymn for St. Ursula & the 11,000 Virgins is what we in the 20th century identify as an incredibly subtle use of the variation principle, in both melody and text. The freedom she achieved thereby was not seen again until our own century when—following the total breakdown of traditional harmony and all the structures it supported—canon and variation were the only purely musical forms remaining, and composers like Schönberg and Webern were once again able to "discover" the structural possibilities of variation.

Daughters of Zion, the new builders of this city which is in unity with itself, and this is a heavenly conception, born of praise and thanksgiving, enwombed in our perpetual virginity.[57]

It is not that I would ever array myself with those of our illustrious Fathers who have spoken out against marriage, for, at its finest and in its ideal, procreation partakes of Creation itself. The seed of the man and the seed of the woman commingle in an act whose issue can be truly creative.[58] Our state, however, is of a higher order; to us is given all of the sensuousness, the nobility, the intentionality of the Heavenly Bridegroom for the daughter who is wooed through her ear,[59] the splendor of the woman clothed in the sun with the moon under her feet as a great sign in heaven (Apocalypse 12). As such, we are graced with the possibility of a higher, spiritual conception, just as Ursula conceived her entire flock and pilgrimage by receiving a divine vision from the Holy Spirit:

> *Honor the Holy Spirit,*
> *Who gathered in the mind of the virgin Ursula*
> *A virginal flock like doves.*
> *Like Abraham she set out,*
> *Leaving her homeland behind,*
> *And just for the loving embrace of the Lamb,*
> *She broke from her chosen betrothed.*[60]

Every day and from all around we see what is begotten physically—the sufferings of birth, the strain of labor, the uncertain state of life itself for the mother, the life in

57. Hildegard refers to the Jerusalem of Vulgate Psalm 121:3: "Jerusalem, which is built as a city, a city that is in unity with itself." Zion, originally the citadel of Jerusalem, by medieval times came to stand for Jerusalem itself as well as the heavenly city of Apocalypse 14:1 and Hebrews 12:22. In Christian religious arts, Zion increasingly comes to stand for the Church on earth; Jerusalem, for the Church in heaven. Hildegard follows a consistent Biblical tradition when, having an eye to her own nuns

perpetuity for the woman subject at all times to the whims and sudden desires of her husband, needing her health and strength for the physical nourishment of a nursing child, her body perhaps required at the same time in the fields for sowing or harvesting spelt, rye, and wheat, for dressing and tying up the tender shoots of grapevines.

With what joy, therefore, are we called by the King for our beauty and chosen to learn all the praises, sing all the offices, cast off our garish clothing to take on the royal nuptial veils with our consecration and vows. With God's help, our spirits, hearts, and minds gradually free themselves for that kind of enlightenment that entered the heart of the Virgin in bearing Her Son, not earthly union but pure conception.

So Ursula conceived both her life and her flock in the light of the Spirit-filled vision she had received, inspiring a pilgrimage of thousands. Her own and other virgins of the Church, she several times identifies Daughters of Zion with the symbolic builders of the city of the Heavenly Jerusalem.

58. Hildegard often comments about the relationship between the physical act of procreation in marriage and that of Creation itself. In her medicophysical treatise *Causae et curae*, she explicitly set forth the process of conception as she understood it: Both men and women have *semen* or seed; when these commingle in intercourse, a child is produced, and the characteristics of that human being vary physically according to the seed, psychological humour, and physical characteristics of each of the marital partners.

59. Hildegard refers to the text of Vulgate Psalm 44, especially verses 11 and 12, "Hearken, O daughter, and see, and incline thy ear: and forget thy people and thy father's house. And the king shall greatly desire thy beauty, for he is the Lord thy God, and him they shall adore." Its twin themes of a young virgin being divinely chosen for her outstanding beauty and excellence, and her refusal of an earthly bridegroom in deference to her passion for Christ, are common to the most revered female saints of the patristic and medieval Church.

60. This is the first full verse with refrain of Hildegard's responsory for St. Ursula & the 11,000 (complete text in Appendix).

individual martyrdom remains a great mystery, but it is clearly joined to the passion of her greatest beloved, Christ the King, about whom she sings:

> *With great yearning*
> *Have I longed to come to you*
> *And to sit at your side*
> *For the heavenly wedding feast,*
> *To stream towards you in a strange way,*
> *Like a cloud which streams sapphire in the purest air.*[61]

So it is that I have been given to birth not one child but twenty-four daughters, unruly, untaught, variously gifted in beauty, in music, in visual and manual dexterity, disobedient nearly all of them, some amenable to learning letters and copying, others trainable enough in needlework or preparation of medicinals, all of them looking to me with mixed emotions as their mother abbess.

And not only women are capable of receiving this God-given gift of spiritual conception: For think of St. Disibode, who isolated himself in total service to God and was used in fact as God's own green finger.[62] He was fecund enough (though only a man) to found a monastery, a monastery fecund enough to house my beloved teacher Jutta, my dearly beloved *magister* and confidant Volmar, to hold out its arms to me and then to other women. Yet Disibode himself maintained his own loneliness in a hermitage apart from his community, not out of pride but out of respect for his vision of the singleness of his service, the absolute need for contemplative

61. This is the third strophe of Hildegard's sequence for St. Ursula & the 11,000 (complete text in Appendix)

62. Hildegard's Responsory for St. Disibode begins, "O you greenness of the finger of God/in whom God planted a vineyard/which shines out in heaven like a column built of light,/you are glorious in your building for God." (*Lieder*, #29, pp. 78–79.)

time, vigilant always against the dangers and allures of the world's demands, even on priests, nuns, abbots, and abbesses.

 The disturbing dreams have returned. Extremities abound. As before, all the responsibility falls to

February 23, 1152

Second Sunday in Lent

me, but this time the obstacles are clearer, as are the details of physical distress. At the beginning of the scene, we are in some kind of a vehicle—perhaps it is the kind of wagon I've seen some of our tenants use on our leased, farmed lands. This time, however, I am the driver. To my right is a wailing infant, incontinent and deeply distressed, as if incontinent at both ends at once. On a back seat is an ancient, tiny, and frail crone, also incontinent, the clothing under her bottom visibly disintegrating from the constant soiling. Others sit among us, but these two are my principal charges—in addition to driving the vehicle. I need perpetually to rearrange these two—the ancient and the infant—and, each time I do this, my hands are soiled by their excreta and the two seem to crumple, to wither in my hands. They are without any internal support; they have no skeletal frame, melting pitifully in and on my hands.

At some point, we are going up a steep incline, the vehicle stops for an obstacle in front of us, and I realize we are sliding backwards down the incline, until it is clear we are about to hit another wagon that is moving behind us. I reach for the stick that should brake the back wheels, and it comes off in my hand. At another point, there are large doors; we are now in an enormous barn and need to drive out, but I cannot find a way to open the doors. They are somehow held closed from the outside, and the operations that will open them elude me completely. Finally, after I have further juggled the dribbling, now crying bodies and sought diligently for a way to maneuver our wagon through the doors, I find myself coming into another building, not a building for animals, but for people. Immediately I come upon a man without a leg, and then one who has so freshly lost his arm that the stump is bloody and ragged, his limb on the floor, his eyes pleading for help. I am shocked that he is upright, able to stand and withstand his wounding.

I awakened to find my own body sore and aching, though not in any of the places specified by the dream that woke me; nevertheless, I am reminded of the torments of my own worst bouts of illness. I remember wondering at that time what the meaning of my suffering was, what the testing was about, and, losing all sense of time and place at times, questioning whether there was any possibility of progression in purgatory. The two barely human, helpless creatures in my dream were so extremely opposed in age, so identical in their pathetic dependency, not on God, but on me. The vehicle, the farm wagon that I cannot brake, can only be driven where it already goes. To try to stop it myself is to cause damage, possibly to slide backwards into oblivion. To slide backwards is unthinkable now that we have finally arrived and won our right to be here. The possibilities for healing and teaching are breathtaking.

Even thinking about the years that went before is to recognize the extreme dependency of our lives as women at Disibodenberg, not so different from that of the infant or the crone of my dream. In truth it is my own demon, this fear of dependency, and in that old dependency the intensification of my debilitation when physical ailments virtually paralyzed me, made any movement impossible, and confined me to bed, totally helpless. Neither could I write nor dictate at those times what was seething inside of me, inaccesssible even to my inner senses. What prayers I could manage were too involved with my will, and it is certainly true that time itself seemed helplessly stuck, that the sharp black ice of February seemed to have encased my body and frozen above my head.

I am here, here with my women, only by the grace of God. The inherent strength of psalms intoned over and over again sustained me in my helplessness, the movement of the inner life invisible to the outer eyes. With this dream, the soiling smells come back, of stale bedding, of sweat-soaked clothing, intensified by the confinement of my cell. Other senses tortured me. Several times my outer vision was rent in two, one jaggedly bordered half having dropped beyond, out of the firmament altogether. When that happened, even to gaze at my then-faithful Rikkarda as she tended me with her gentle eyes was to risk seeing only one-half of her face; the other disappeared as if into a vacuum, I wishing desperately to touch with my fingers, to test and see if there was something palpable taken from my field of vision that could still be known through other natural senses; fearful that, if I did so, and my touch merely confirmed what my eyes didn't see, I would know myself for a madwoman.[63]

The cold clang of the bell, Vespers, and the Magnificat.

March 9, 1152
Fourth Sunday in Lent

 Three stones fell this morning as they were completing the archway for the west portal. The noise was deafening. In our still-unfinished choir we were singing Prime, and, as the Divine Office was torn into tatters with the sound, I thought immediately about the stone that was rejected: Christ the noble *lapis* who forms with His own body the cornerstone of the holy city.[64] Apparently we have no proper cornerstone for that archway, I

63. One of the most frightening symptoms reported by people who suffer from migraine is the experience of temporarily having whole sections of their field of vision torn away, as Hildegard describes. Several medical scientists have posited the possibility that Hildegard suffered throughout her life from a chronic migraine condition. Their evidence is based on the scotomata of the miniatures painted to illustrate the visions of *Scivias* and her descriptions of recurrent episodes of chronic suffering. (See Sacks, *Migraine*, ch. 3, and Singer, *Magic*, ch. 6.)

64. Hildegard detailed her vision of Christ as the cornerstone of the wall of the Heavenly Jerusalem in the second vision, Book II of her *Scivias*. A painted illumination for this vision shows Christ literally woven into the ninety-degree angle of two stone walls; an excellent color reproduction of this miniature is in Führkotter, *Miniatures*, plate 21.

thought, but my master builder said, no, it wasn't the keystone at all, and showed me that the damage was minimal. The three stones that fell were not structurally important, but were merely facing for surface. What's important is the portal itself, the door that leads to the area where the baptismal font will stand. I cherish the hope of having the font in the form of a pelican for baptisms by Easter.

The pelican is such a complex creature, a bird I've never seen, a creature of waste places, as we are reminded again and again in the penitential psalm that will lead us into the last three days of Holy Week. "I am become like a pelican of the wilderness,"[65] cries the psalmist. The nobility of such a creature is isolate; its voice, rarely heard, is like that of the Baptist himself, a voice crying in the wilderness.[66] If we could, as Adam before the Fall, hear all the sounds in the universe, all the hummings of earth and the music of the spheres, would the sound of the pelican be as the call to baptism? In part, it must be the voice of the primordial, cleansing waters. And the music of water will be ever varied, from the first sound of the snow-melted spring freshet that swells the mountain brooks in the woods on the Rupertsberg, to the meandering flow of our lazy River Nahe, the joining of it with the grander Rhine, and all the way to the great oceans that surround the earth and support the firmament. So for the noble pelican there are all these watery varieties of sound in its music, plus the sound of its lonely stance, its brooding silences, and even the rhythm of these brooding silences.

No less important is the half-forgotten female nature of this creature of the Nile. St. Augustine, great teacher of the Church, has in a sense rebaptized for us in Christian vestment the ancient pagan story of the pelican as the one whose young will time and again poke

65. Vulgate Psalm 101:7. Verses from Psalm 101 are used liturgically in great variety during Holy Week. For example, different verses are used as texts for the Tract, the Offertory, and the Communion chants at the Mass for Wednesday in Holy Week.

66. John 1:19–23.

at its breast and eyes until their own deaths must result, but whose mother-blood, pulled in sorrow from its breast with its own beak, then serves to restore their lives. Such is the creator bird, the Holy Spirit, the brooding bird who carries the *Ruach*, the terrifying roar and rush of primal waters, the bird who broods over the creation in Genesis as upon a clutch of eggs that must be brought to being with the life-giving warmth of her own breast.[67] And breath! I hear the sounds of God's *spiraculo*, breathing life into what is otherwise clay and only of deep earth.[68] The breath of life, and of singing praise, and of music-making for the glory of God, in harmony with the music of the heavenly spheres, even though we may not be able to hear them clearly in these fallen and corrupted times. Underneath all the texts, all the sacred psalms and canticles, these watery varieties of sounds and silences, terrifying, mysterious, whirling and sometimes gestating and gentle must somehow be felt in the pulse, ebb, and flow of the music that sings in me. My new song must float like a feather on the breath of God.[69]

67. Newman (*Sister of Wisdom*, pp. 190–91) discusses this variant, sapiential reading of the Creation in chapter 1 of Genesis, and the revival in the 12th century of the "ancient notion of the Annunciation as a second Genesis." In commenting on the text "but already, over the waters, brooded the Spirit of God," Peter Abelard in 1135 wrote, "Therefore, just as the bird brooding on the egg and devoting herself to it with extreme ardour warms it with her own heat, forms the chicken and brings it to life, so divine goodness…is said to be set over that still fluid and unstable mass as over waters, that presently it might bring forth living creatures from it…" (*Expositio in Hexameron*, trans. Dronke in *Fabula*, pp. 95–96.)

68. The notion of human life infusing clay or earth is from Genesis 2:7, "And now from the clay of the ground, the Lord God formed man, breathed into his nostrils the breath of life, and made man a living soul." A relationship between music and breath is reflected linguistically in the derivation of the word "neume" (notational symbol) from the Greek word for breath, *pneuma*.

69. Hildegard several times uses the image of a feather on the breath of God when referring to herself, in much

So I give thanks that we have found in Fulbert, our master mason, a man who can carve the noble pelican, bring it into its shape, even with the motherly breast that supports the basin itself. As a lay brother, borrowed from the Cistercian house of Rievaulx,[70] he surprised me with his love for the three-dimensional forms of sculpture, so frowned upon in Cistercian houses but not to be despised for their beauty in shape and texture. He and I have talked often enough that I am assured of his deep understanding of these mysteries, even within his seeming rusticity of speech. His gift is in his hands, in their connection to his simple heart. His work with stone is a contemplative act, a prayer that discovers and connects every curve and color of the mineral-laced stone he has found for the purpose. Three catechumens will be ready for baptism at the Easter Vigil[71] this year, in the shadow of the cross from the font of the pelican.

In less than three months' time, even before Ascen-

the same way as she uses the image of a trumpet or mouthpiece of God in order to illustrate the way she is used as an instrument of the divine in all her human, womanly, bodily weakness. For example, "But I am always filled with a trembling fear, as I do not know for certain of any single capacity in me. Yet I stretch out my hands to God, so that, like a feather which lacks all weight and strength and flies through the wind, I may be borne up by him." (Trans. Dronke, *WWMA*, p. 168.)

70. Rievaulx, a monastery in England, was made famous through the writings of Aelred, its third abbot (1147–67). Typical of the ideals of the Cistercian reform of the 12th century, it was located in remote, wild countryside, its architecture extremely plain, and its economic success due to good agricultural practices and careful raising of sheep.

71. Catechumens, those who were being taught as preparation for baptism, were not allowed to participate in the Eucharist, or central action of the Mass, until their baptism. In medieval times, baptism was administered at only a few important feast days; principal among these was Holy Saturday, as part of the Paschal Vigil, where it enjoyed the rich symbolism of light and water in the surrounding texts.

sion Day, Archbishop Henry of Mainz will come to consecrate our cloister church. He and I are deeply in disagreement over the appointment of Rikkarda; our church will not be finished, but our baptisms will be accomplished and heard.

 For once they took me at my word when I insisted on not being interrupted during the work period between Sext and None.

March 16, 1152
Passion Sunday and Fifth
Sunday in Lent

Had I known the extent of the man's pain or how frightening to him the visual excitations that accompanied it, I would have taken time from dictating to Volmar and put hands on immediately. The shape of his head was visibly distorted; that and his intermittent raving, describing the searing lights that were tearing across his visual field, finally prompted the infirmarian to come after me. His eyes were unusually dark, with no visible pupils at the center; one eye looked warily off to the side with darting movements. He was heavyset, determined, and intelligent looking, clearly in prayer at the moment I first observed him and unmindful of being observed.

First I needed to determine whether this could possibly be another case of possession. It's not that charms or even exorcisms are too difficult for us, but the forces of evil are devious in the extreme; they may lie and feint and are full of treachery. It is important that they be recognized and named. In them there is a murky presence, an almost palpable cloud in which they carry their being, and I am getting better at knowing when they are there. Unacknowledged, they could even enter my own person: I must invoke God's protection for myself and my community, but especially, these days, for my own person. I still can't be sure whether my extreme physical relapse two years ago might not have been occasioned by the unrecognized demons in the possessed woman at Disibodenberg. My physical symptoms at the time so imitated hers. By not naming them, rather than dissipating the cloudy presence I may have eliminated her symptoms by taking on her demons, allowing their vapors to soak into my being in unaware obedience until it was far too late. This phenomenon is a possibility even in the absence of demons, and can happen with any extreme symptoms of illness that I am able to heal with prayer and the laying on of hands; but the control it exerts over me is much greater in the case of possession, because that involves the invasion of soul as well as body.

In the case of the dark young man, it became clear that it was not possession; his reason and thinking faculties were his own. His senses were distorted by the degree of pain and fear his symptoms were causing. As I stood in front of him, he suddenly bowed his head, and the huge swelling at the edge of his skull on the lower left protruded even through the mass of dark, wiry hair. I wondered about his coloring and that intent density in his eyes: for a moment I thought him a Saracen. But he was clearly at prayer, and his heavy lips moved quickly. As I came close enough to apply my right hand to the swollen knob on the lower edge of his skull, I heard the rhythms of his prayer. It was not Latin.

I suppose a silent *Pater noster* is what I was saying as I began to get the first hint of change in the swollen protuberance, and, although I could tell from the movements in his body that the reduction in swelling was causing him some sharp pain in the immediate area, I didn't let up at all on the intention I sent through my hands until I could feel that the swelling was reduced. Then, with the fingers of my left hand half an inch or more above the surface of the rough mustard-colored wool shirt that covered his upper body, I quickly scanned his back as he sat looking away from me. The area around his heart was clearly warmer than anything else, and I anchored my right hand there. It felt more and more that my right palm was receiving something—it tingled and trembled—and I let all my attention go into the filling of that palm as I continued my prayers and he continued his, although his sounds were still unrecognizable to me. It occurred to me then that he might be chanting Hebrew.

When the crisis was over, his body temperature uniform, and the two sides of his skull nearly identical, I asked the infirmarian to stop bustling around us, and we had a few minutes to talk. En route to his community down the Rhine, he explained, he had been struck from his mount by a sudden attack of illness, and his companion had convinced townspeople from Bingen to bring him, nearly unconscious, through our gate. His gratitude at the relief of pain and symptoms precluded any deception about his identity, and I learned he was a Jew, a scholar of the Torah and student of the mysteries of something he identified as Kabbalah. His knowledge of patriarchs and prophets was vast; his curiosity about the more arcane knowledge to be gained through contemplation of certain symbols (one of them in the figure of a cross) in connection with Kabbalah was intriguing. I asked him to chant some of his Hebrew prayers aloud, and the music was different from anything I had previously heard. It was high, on the edge, and he sang through the nasal passages in a way that gave it a kind of insistence; this, coupled with frank and exact repetitions, made the sound almost instrumental and hypnotic, like a tiny reed with air, words, and peculiar rhythms pushing themselves through with very great effort.

He then told me that he had suffered the one-sided swelling in his skull before, and that it was always accompanied by excruciating pains behind both eyes. His outer vision became greatly impaired. Showers of stars raced across his inner vision; they were of a gold so glittering that the entire inner surface of his skull felt bruised by the charge of their motion and brightness. Sometimes these showers would suddenly darken, blacken really, and whole sections of the air they filled would tear off and disappear, as if part of some horrifying void had swallowed up the overbright, sparkling activity. His fear as he described these things was very apparent; his breathing was eruptive, and it was difficult to calm him. I understood what he was describing, and I knew in my heart that something about this poor Jew's painful apparitions was holy. They were from God the Father, just as my visions are from the Holy Spirit through the Voice of Wisdom. Perhaps the extreme distortions of his head and eyes were caused by his fear at seeing with his inner senses, by his not being able to accept the depth from which his experience sprang. His heart is closed to Christ and Ecclesia, but in relation to his people he could be a prophet who must master his fear and teach.

He will stay with us for a few days.

 Another vision came, unexpectedly, this time through the beech tree. Crossing the cloister after Matins to March 21, 1152 Feast of St. Benedict make a brief visit to the makeshift dispensary to tend the suffering in predawn silence, I feel aerial spirits circulate damp anguish blocking my freedom to move about with any fluidity at all, and wonder when I can once again insist upon Matins at its proper middle-of-the-night time without defections on every side. Add the grumblings and threatened defections of my women so used to the well-endowed comforts at Disibodenberg who find such barrenness here, knowing nothing of the potential our community holds. And now, just as we receive new deeds to productive farms and future vineyards that make our lives promising enough for me to proceed with things like carrying away the dirty water in the Roman way,[72] the rude letter comes demanding my beloved Rikkarda, and I can hardly think.[73]

72. Guibert of Gembloux, Hildegard's last secretary and scribe, attested to the remarkable facilites he found in her convent, including the unusal feature of running water in all the workshops (excerpt of letter in Neuls-Bates, *Women in Music*, pp. 11–12).

73. Hildegard probably refers here to the letter she received from Henry, archbishop of Mainz, advising her that he was sending escorts for Rikkarda who would accompany her to her new post. Although this made further protest futile, it did not prevent the abbess from responding with a sharp, admonitory letter to the archbishop that warns him about the buying and selling of offices and about the particularly short-lived reign and

And yet the music sings in me, comes when least I would have it. Crossing the cloister at dawn, barely any peach-orangey-rose in the sky at all, certainly not any that would rise above the cloister wall at this hour and season; and yet the light appears, and of such a saturated shade it begins to acquire an odor of late-March earth as well. Hyacinths and crocus bulbs planted only last fall, nestling into the bases of our dun walls, push up thickly green. My eye follows their path of bloom and bud, spirals within the barely greening patches of earth thawed within the cloister, and, in the Shadow of the Living Light, the giant beech tree is suddenly transformed, and she is there before me as a tree and speaks with the Voice of Wisdom. Her whole torso takes on the strong contours of the beech trunk, but whose bark is patterned in plates and scales, as of a giant fish. I am acutely aware of my hands, their tingling almost to itchiness, and I place them first on the smooth trunk, then gently cupped to my ears, knowing the connection between us needs to be sounded into more being. I hardly dare raise my eyes, knowing the sudden brightness that will be generated, knowing it will at first make me dizzy and lightheaded although its energy is always welcome. But it isn't the Blessed Virgin, after all. There is no nest in her hair. Nor do birds nest in her, or sing.[74] It is my beloved Ursula, and hers is a very different sound. She is herself the size of the tree, crowned as Ecclesia. She requires that we sing a new song,[75] that my virgins and widows sing, and we will celebrate her feast this October with offices of her making; but this song will be more than Office music, this is the sequence for the Eucharistic feast itself, and Volmar will celebrate with it, feeling its power in us, allowing it to soar above the Propers and Ordinaries

fate of Nebuchadnezzar, another powerful man whom God cast from his throne for his pride and rash decisions (*PL*, pp. 156–57).

74. See Hildegard's "*O viridissima virga*" (O greenest branch), in Lieder, #71, pp. 146–48. English text by author in *Signs*, V, 3, p. 566.

75. Vulgate Psalm 95:1 begins, "Sing to the Lord a new song (*canticum novum*): sing to the Lord, all the earth."

that surround it.[76] She will have her day. Below the waist, her trunk is silver like the beech itself but shiny, very shiny. Above the waist she is both strangely armless and as having many, many arms of bright gold, emanating like the calyx of a lotus whose efflorescence is her own crowned head; some of the sepals over her breasts hold throngs of people—patriarchs, prophets, but most of all women, all of them bright and beautiful, bright and beautiful, all of them gifted with sound, and singing like great, wild birds.[77]

The bell calls me to Lauds.

March 23, 1152
Palm Sunday

 I went into the Great Silence hearing the sound of Rikkarda's voice practicing "*Cum fabricator mundi*" [When the Maker of the world] as we had gone over it together so many times in the past. I cannot imagine that even the papal *schola cantorum*[78] can manage the piece except soloistically. The long, long lines are as brutal to sustain as the events it narrates, and it is powerful the way she has learned to deliver it.[79] It

76. In medieval times, the five parts of the Mass sung identically each day by the whole congregation or community are *Kyrie, Gloria, Credo, Sanctus,* and *Agnus dei.* The five parts sung by the *schola,* whose texts vary with each day of the liturgical year, are Introit, Gradual, Alleluia or Tract, Offertory, and Communion.

77. Führkotter, *Miniatures,* pl. 14 renders this visionary image in color, identified as *Mater Ecclesia.* (In Hildegard's lexicon of iconic women, Ecclesia, Caritas (Love), Sapientia, the Virgin, and Ursula sometimes become conflated in their functions and appearances.)

78. Technical term referring to a small group of singers, drawn from the community, dedicated to the study and performance of liturgical music, especially chant. The most difficult music would be assigned to the *schola,* or even to individual cantors within it.

79. The antiphon Hildegard names above was part of the Good Friday liturgy until the 15th century of the cosmos. It narrates in gory detail the cataclysmic response of the cosmos (rending of the veil of the temple, opening of graves, and an earthquake) to Christ's crucifixion, followed by a shimmering, lyrical meditation on the spiritual meaning of the events (Blackley, "Music for Holy

makes me hopeful that even now something will happen to change their minds, so that she will sing it for us on Good Friday—that I can save my voice for the Lamentations this last week and concentrate my teaching energies on the difficult Matins responsories.[80]

My inner senses are always open to the sights that God will reveal to me, my ears alert to the Voice of Wisdom, but the blessings of the Great Silence are particularly rich, and it is then that I most often receive and shape my new music, Daughter of Zion rejoice! Last evening during the Silence, Ecclesia appeared to me in her *Exultet* form, adorned in dazzling light[81] and quite beautifully confounded with both the queen bee and the Paschal candle itself.[82]

Week"). Like Hildegard's Sequence for St. Ursula & the 11,000 Virgins, its music moves freely over a range of thirteen pitches (a wider range than usual in chant) and was probably sung by a solo cantor from the *schola*. In a remote, nearly autonomous women's monastery, the likelihood is that both the "*Cum fabricator*" antiphon for Good Friday and the "*O Ecclesia*" sequence for Ursula (sung following the Alleluia of the Mass on October 21st) would have been sung by Hildegard herself or by her chief cantrix.

🔹 80. In medieval religious communities, Holy Week was arduous. Fasting was intensified and a great deal of additional music had to be learned, since every syllable of text was sung each day, including at the last those texts of the long Paschal Vigil which accompanied the Blessing of the New Fire, lighting of the Easter candle, and baptism of catechumens. The texts of the Matins responsories Hildegard mentions above were originally taken from the Biblical Lamentations of Jeremiah.

🔹 81. The *Exultet*, a prose-poem written perhaps by Ambrose, the great 4th-century bishop of Milan, is chanted (usually by a deacon) at the beginning of the Paschal Vigil. Ecclesia is the third in a trinity evoked therein, following the rejoicing of the heavenly host and that of the earth: "Let Mother Church also rejoice, adorned as she now is in dazzling light; and let this building resound with the joyful voices of God's people." Thus is established the theological theme of the ancient Paschal Vigil, not the agony of crucifixion, but the cosmic rejoicing sounded to mark the triumph of light in the darkness, prefigured in the Passover.

🔹 82. "But this is enough of the glory of this candle: the

In the vision, the bees began at a great distance, so far away that I could barely hear them. Without alarm, I remembered how bees can relieve chronic pain in joints and tissues where they sting, how the controlled use of the bee sting is both a penetration and a healing. But these bees were swarming, and there were thousands of them. In the Shadow of the Living Light I watched them circling the trees, approaching like an undulating cloud whose shape changed in swirls from within, like the woven texture of a tapestry that repatterns and reweaves itself from within ever-changing borders.

They arrived at an orchard, which was also a cemetery, beautifully planted with fruit-bearing trees, thirteen fruit trees, arranged around a hawthorn tree so covered with white blossoms it was dazzling to the eye. Fourteen burial plots were arranged symmetrically, seven and seven, those fruit trees between them bright with blooming flowers in shades of rose and peach.[83] The buzzing sound becomes painfully loud as they swarm into the orchard; then suddenly the huge swarm divides itself into thirteen spiraling smaller swarms, lacing themselves around the branches of each of the blossoming fruit trees. In the center, a domed honeycomb emerges out of the hawthorn tree, golden wings threading through and out of it, Ecclesia's crown below it, the whole encased in a shimmering aureole of

glowing flame kindles it in God's honour. Even if the flame is shared by others, it loses nothing of its brightness, for it is always fed by the melting wax, which the mother bee brought forth to be the substance of this wonderful light." (From chant of the *Exultet*, as above.)

▨ 83. In the overall design of a medieval monastery, it is not uncommon for the orchard and cemetery to share common ground. (For a projected, illustrated plan, see Price, *Plan of St. Gall*, p. 67.)

▨ 84. This is one of two responsories Hildegard wrote for the Feast of St. Ursula & the 11,000 Virgins. Note the similarity of language (its first line derived from a line of the Song of Songs) to that of an antiphon for the Feast of St. Agnes, used as well for the Ceremony for the Consecration of a Virgin: "Honey and milk have I received from his mouth, and his blood has adorned my cheeks."

light. Ecclesia, the queen bee, is dripping honey and milk. The bees in the thirteen trees become women, holy virgins, perched among the branches; the blossoms become garlands, rosy diadems for each head; the queen emerges as Ursula.

At first the swarm of women is only buzzing, but once she fully occupies the center, once the dome of the hive clearly houses Ursula the queen, yellow liquid paths of honey and undulating ribbons of wax begin to connect them as in a dance. Its smell is overpowering—the pungent odor of balsam.

It ends abruptly; I find I am dripping with sweat, from the movement of the molten matrix, the warmth of the new fire, the pillar of light, this birth of the Paschal candle itself. Sounds begin to differentiate themselves, slow and condensed as if starting from the enflamed gathered place of the central dome. It is clear to me how it moves and where the words go:

> *A dripping honeycomb*
> *Was the virgin Ursula*
> *Who longed to embrace the Lamb of God.*
> *Honey and milk under her tongue,*
> *Because she gathered to herself*
> *A fruit-bearing garden and the most fragrant flowers*
> *   in a swarm of virgins.*
> *Therefore, Daughter of Zion, rejoice*
> *   in this most golden dawn!*
> *Because she gathered to herself*
> *A fruit-bearing garden and the most fragrant flowers*
> *   in a swarm of virgins.*
> *Glory be to the Father and to the Son*
> *And to the Holy Spirit.*
> *Because she gathered to herself*
> *A fruit-bearing garden and the most fragrant flowers*
> *   in a swarm of virgins.*[84]

Huge crows and raucous star-
lings descend ravenously on
the newly plowed fields. Their

March 25, 1152

Feast of the Annunciation

Lenten fare is juicier than ours, as two of the sisters remind me. The cows and goats have yet to freshen, and so we are temporarily out of milk at the end of Lent; the cellaress receives these complaints and hunts for other sources nearby.

Although the moon is full and in the water sign of Scorpio, planting of herbs is not favorable during Holy Week,[85] and—until our own lands are more productive of medicinals and foodstuffs—we still lack the real autonomy that will finally preclude depen-
dence on other people's harvests, especially those at Disibodenberg. I fear that the wrenching disruptions of our breaking away have made wounds that are slow to heal, even after two years. My persistent tenac-
ity about retaining my dear secretary Volmar as our provost and priest was a crucial issue, and just as threatening to Abbot Kuno as our winning the lands for the Rupertsberg and being granted permission for the establishment of our community from the See at Mainz.[86]

85. In the 20th century, as first revived in Rudolf Steiner's concepts of biodynamic gardening, farmers have again begun to consider the effects of the phases and positions of moon and planets on organic growth. In liturgical calendars of the 12th century, astrological-astronomical information was always included and was an essential part of the computation of the date of Easter each year, upon which the dates of all movable feasts of the Church turned.

86. An autobiographical fragment from Hildegard's *Vita* tells us, "And in accordance with what I perceived in my true vision, I said to the Father Abbot: 'The serene light says: You shall be father to our provost, and father of the salvation of the souls of the daughters of my mystic garden. But their alms do not belong to you or to your brothers—your cloister should be a refuge for these women. If you are determined to go on with your perverse proposals, raging against us, you will be like the Amalekites, and like Antiochus, of whom it was written that he despoiled the Temple of the Lord. If some of

We still sing badly in choir much of the time, gradually weaning ourselves from what I scarcely realized was a sort of moral support for our sound that came from our brothers in Christ at Disibodenberg. Our psalms are ragged. Nevertheless, our singing improves, and my women begin to live according to the Rule as it has been shown to me. They are starting to have a feel for the psalm tones and cadences as I lead them. My hand indicates the rhythm and shape of each rise and fall, at the same time informing the musical line with a wholeness, and the ancient Biblical texts take on some passionate meaning when they are pointed correctly.

Perhaps the songs I have written in honor of St. Disibode will help salve the wounds of my old abbot; I was encouraged when I heard his response, which he sent last week with Br. Andrew. Not only is he pleased with the sequence for Disibode, he is eager for antiphons and responsories for the feast as well: "If they should come to you, I would be pleased to have such music in the Divine Office that day for our patron saint."[87] I hear these as generous and forgiving words, unless Br. Andrew took the rougher edges from his abbot's message and embellished them with gold out of his own sorrow for our damaged, and undeservedly bad, reputation among them.

I remember, once in the old days at St. Disibode's [Disibodenberg], foraging for early plants with Rikkarda, both of us fairly smeared with and smothered by the smells of the herbs

you, unworthy ones, said to yourselves: Let's take some of their freeholds away— then I WHO AM say: You are the worst of robbers. And if you try to take away the shepherd of spiritual medicine [i.e., Provost Volmar], then again I say, you are sons of Belial, and in this do not look to the justice of God. So that same justice will destroy you.'

"And when I, poor little creature *(paupercula forma)*, had with these words petitioned the abbot and his confreres for the freehold of the site and domains of my daughters, they all granted it to me, entering the transfer in a codex." (Trans. Dronke, *WWMA*, p. 153.)

87. Paraphrase of part of letter from Abbot Kuno to Hildegard, *PL*, p. 203.

and simples of spring on that noble mountainside heaving up out of the broad valleys around. I dizzy easily in its contemplation; my head and inner senses flood with insistent light. I am filled with the figure of Disibode in the responsory: He sings himself as the greening of God's finger, transforming the entire mountain from a bleached-out, barren cone into its fructification as the plantation of God. Even the sounds center and descend from above, starting not from a resting place, but descending out of the hand of God from the reciting tone of the mode, as the green creative finger refuses to rest.[88]

When our mountains first turn fully green, I know that the Resurrection is with us renewed. No wonder that the Holy Land is always green, that Jerusalem is never cold, barren, or dulled like our Lenten Februarys, when the stretching light is the only hope. Or the deception of our entire month of March, when a day may begin with fresh odors and birdcalls, only to bring gale winds, freezing, rutted roads, and blinding flurries of snow. Horrid, bleak expanses, were it not for the promise of Gabriel's Annunciation on this very day.

I hear lambing sounds, and so it goes with most of the peasant women of Bingen, such regular yearly birthings; but not so for Guidelbert last night, gray with loss of blood when she arrived at our door, carried by a kinsman ignorant of ways of retrieving the afterbirth and too terrified at the sight of the monster-child that was to have been her first. Mother of God, speak to me! Tiny daggers of ice ring my joints, still swaddled this late in the year with woolen cloths. How I long for the honey-warmth in my limbs! At least the sun climbs high enough to enter the casement for the office of Lauds, so that the whole interior of the choir was illuminated for Lauds of the Annunciation. At First Vespers last night our pans of paper-white narcissus incensed the space with their

88. Hildegard refers to the responsory she wrote for St. Disibode (*Lieder*, #29, pp. 76–77), in which the music does not obey the customary rules of modal writing for the 12th century; instead, the melody follows the contour of the text in a kind of word painting.

starry blooms—the heat of the sun having increased their moisture and perfume as we framed the fourth and fifth psalms with two of my most beloved antiphons: "Now the winter is past, the rains are over and gone; arise, my beloved, and come!" and "You are beautiful and sweet in your delights, holy Mother of God."

And when the hand of God comes each spring to touch our Rupertsberg lands, dozens of different shades of green sculpt whole curved sections into the faces of our mountains: emerald ovals of meadow grass, looking shaved from this distance, where the sheep can once again leave our shelter safely to graze; faces of cliffs dotted with shimmering clumps of wet moss and newly sprouting gray-green of wild columbine waiting to unfold whorls of juxtaposed yellow and orange trumpeting tubes; and deeply forested patches of pine and balsam that never entirely lose their green, except as it dulls in the meagerly lighted days surrounding the winter solstice. Our Paschal Vigil may take us into bright April some Easters: Then the glory of the renewed Christ illuminates those other stands of great trees. Their skeletons have stood ugly brown to winter blasts, exposed to chilling swaths of snow and repeated girdlings of ice, desolate of all birds except the occasional preying hawk or owl. April is theirs, as fat, waxy leaf buds continue to moisten and swell in their first appearance, like burnished minerals with sheened colors of copper, garnet, and bronze. Finally in May—after the ferns have all uncurled, the shaved meadows stabilized their green two shades darker, all the corms, bulbs, and tubers have blossomed so that our eyes have been taken by a dazzling array of color close at hand—we suddenly notice that catkins have already come and tasseled each twig, that the explosion of maple and oak, birch, and beech can blaze their paths through, up, and around the mountain slopes, even around our own arable fields and fruit-bearing meadows, processing up to our very portal and surrounding us like a bird-infested sanctuary of green.

My portress today received a priest and colleague of Volmar who talks of hearing several remarkable sermons by Bernard of Clairvaux, sermons turning on his contemplation of the *mulier amicta sole* from the Apocalypse, the woman clothed in the sun with the moon under her feet, and with twelve stars on her head for a crown; pregnant, and in labor, crying aloud in the pangs of childbirth.[89] My women need to understand that there are other labors and birthings besides those we observe among the peasants of Bingen. Volmar agrees with me that we need readings like this at Chapter and even in the refectory to augment writings from the Church Fathers;[90] perhaps a section of one of Bernard's sermons about the woman clothed in the sun can serve as a lesson for a Nocturn in Matins during the Octave of Pentecost, though I doubt we could possibly have it soon enough with the roads flooded out.

March 26, 1152
Wednesday in Holy Week

 Ite missa est. Rikkarda left on Sunday with the dismissal,[91] having done her confession with Volmar; he was therefore the last to share her private sounds and prayers and was too busy—otherwise occupied—to come to the aid of the old abbess, to work out the thousand details for this day, let alone the next ones in this endless agonizing week. And who now besides myself can sing the Lamentations for Thursday's Matins?[92] She could already be in place by Friday, to preside in her own house, to witness with her nuns the disintegrating of the liturgy

89. Book of Apocalypse 12:1 and 2.

90. Chapter denotes a meeting of the members of a religious community, its name originating in the practice of reading an appropriate chapter of the Rule at each meeting. The refectory is where nuns and monks eat their meals, which are silent activities for everyone except the person who reads aloud to the community.

91. The final words at Mass, sung by the priest from the altar, are, "Go, you are dismissed." This is the source of the common term *missa* (Mass) for the Eucharistic feast.

92. The Lamentations of Jeremiah are an important part of the liturgy on Thursday, Friday, and Saturday of Holy Week. The laments, each verse of which begins with a letter of the Hebrew alphabet, are chanted by a solo cantor.

that day—the chilling absence of Eucharist, the chanting of John's account, the betrayal, his heartbroken Passion.[93]

But the Passions are for Volmar to chant: long, arduous, and exhausting as it was on Sunday when she left, when he had to do it completely without the young deacon from Mainz, who may yet arrive to assist him today; or else he may not, and Volmar, like me, will sing alone in his own loneliness. He who is my dear *magister*, my own *symmista*,[94] won as my own personal secretary and attendant, spent these last days with her when I should have been the one to prepare her for the position, answer her questions and insecurities about the office like a wise abbess and good mother. Clearly, I was unable. The physical symptoms have returned with intensity, and care for my own flock —the ones still loyal— must be first for me, to lead them praising through His death and resurrection with whatever diminished strength remains.

The Mass for Holy Wednesday is filled with wretchedness: Psalm 101 at Offertory and Communion[95] can be sung by the choir, but the Tract before Luke's Passion is my own solo; thereto I add my

93. Accounts of Christ's Passion are assigned to certain days in Holy Week: Palm Sunday, according to Matthew (26:36–27:60); Tuesday, according to Mark (14:32–15:46); Wednesday, according to Luke (22:39–23:53); Friday, according to John (18:1–19:42). On Good Friday there is no Mass, with its mystical presence of Christ in the Eucharist, but only the dramatic, staged presence of His death. It is as if the liturgy, whose form was already weakened on Holy Thursday, has stumbled to a complete halt. Nor is there a Mass during Holy Saturday—only, late at night, the Paschal Vigil, in which the rudiments of the Mass form may again be found. The liturgy returns to its full glory Easter Sunday morning.

94. *Magister* (master) is a medieval Latin term of academic rank, still in use today, indicating that part of Volmar's role which was teacher. The Latin word *symmista*, on the other hand, means a colleague in a sacred office, indicating the ways in which Hildegard considered Volmar an equal in their relationship.

95. The text for the Offertory with its verses (℣.): "Hear my prayer, O Lord, and let my cry

own wretchedness and let it be cradled by the crying misery of the psalmist: ‡‡*O Lord, hear my prayer and let my cry come unto thee.* ℣. *Do not turn thy face away from me, but lend me thy ear in time of affliction.* ℣. *Give me swift audience whenever I call upon thee.* ℣. *See how this life of mine passes away like smoke, how this face wastes as if melted in an oven.* ℣. *Drained of strength like grass the sun scorches, I leave my food untasted, forgotten.* ℣. *Surely thou wilt bestir thyself, Lord, and give Zion redress: it is time now to take pity on her.*[96] ‡‡

Before Vespers

 Still this day goes on and is beyond relief. It is dry beyond belief, with no water at all. There are no tears. Texts catch in my jaws, the pitches in my throat, filled with dust and ashes. Bitter thoughts line my brain. Who and how am I, to wash the feet of any tomorrow, the first day of the Great Triduum?[97]

March 27, 1152
Thursday in Holy Week

 It is nearly time for Matins, and everything in my own body seems to be breaking down and pulling apart. The Great Triduum is upon us, and I am bent and

come unto thee. ℣. For I have forgotten to eat my bread. ℣. Thou wilt bestir thyself, and give Zion redress; it is time now to take pity on her, for the time has come." For the Communion: "I drink nothing but what comes to me mingled with my tears, so low thou hast brought me, who didst once lift me so high; I waste away like grass in the sun: Lord, thou endurest for ever: surely thou wilt bestir thyself, and give Zion redress: it is time now to take pity on her."

▨ 96. Vulgate Psalm 101:2–5 and 14.

▨ 97. Hildegard refers to the traditional Washing of the Feet on Holy Thursday, when it is common in monastic houses for the abbot or abbess to wash the feet of those in his or her charge, in imitation of Christ's washing the feet of His disciples.

▨ 98. Text from Matins for Holy Thursday, the response to Lesson iii at First Nocturn; derived from Lamentations of Jeremiah 1:10–14.

▨ 99. This antiphon is sung after verses of the ancient responsorial hymn "*Crux fidelis*" (Faithful Cross) and is part of the Liturgy of Good Friday.

spent under this burden of loss and what feels like betrayal. No one cares for these old bones and tired throat. Washing and wailing are what are required. For Jeremiah, to be a bird, to be only a winged singer, is how to get through. The Lamentations are mine: ‡‡ Jod. *The enemy has stretched out his hand over all her precious things: yea, she has seen that the nations invade her sanctuary, whom you forbade to enter your congregation.* Caph. *All her people groan, they seek bread: they trade their treasures for food to revive their strength: see, O Lord, and consider; for I am become vile.* Lamed. *Is it nothing to you, all you who pass by? Behold, and see if there is any sorrow like my sorrow, which was brought upon me, which the Lord inflicted on the day of his fierce anger.* Mem. *From on high he sent fire; into my bones he made it descend. He spread a net for my feet, he turned me back; he has left me stunned and faint all the day.* Nun. *The yoke of my transgressions is bound by his hand; they were fastened together, and set upon my neck; he caused my strength to fail, the Lord gave me into the hands of those whom I cannot withstand. Jerusalem, Jerusalem, return unto the Lord your God.* [98] ‡‡

March 28, 1152
Friday in Holy Week

ANTIPHON TO THE HYMN: [99]
Faithful Cross, of trees created,
Noblest tree of all art thou,
Forest none bears trees as thou art,
Like in leaf, or flower, or bough.
Dear the nails, and dear the timber:
Dear the load they bear aloft.

The cloister garden has begun to bloom, but it has been planted so far with little regard

April 6, 1152
First Sunday after Easter

for the final shapes and colors it may assume. Simply filling in spaces, as we did at Disibodenberg, no longer proves practical or pleasing; we, like the garden, must create our own rhythms and patterns within the ordered strictures of the Rule. Two more hillsides have been given to us and three promised. The Cistercian success with viniculture could be ours as well, and the handsome diagonal stripes on the curving bellysides of the Nahe speak of salts and rocks, minerals fertile to the cuttings we plant. Who knows what wonderfully bouqueted wine our own riverbanks may in time produce? Mists perpetually hiding in the clefts of these hills on April mornings promise moisture, and so we need not fear the aridity of parched earth as a growing medium.

Our enclosed cloister gardens should serve us as well. Already the wild April meadows yield green herbs for our table, and these not without colorful blossoms; the yellow mustards and gentians also provide poultices and tonics. Intense cultivation can yield the medicinal herbs to staunch wounds, ease joints, relieve congestion, not only for our own new house, but for those who inevitably seek hospice here, just as they did at St. Disibode's. Our healing skills are known in the area even though we are not fully established; we are sought out by individuals as diverse as peasant women with complications of birthing and the student of Talmud and Kabbalah so recently in my care. Lord knows how we will house them all—travelers needing temporary, safe shelter or those who are desperate for nursing attention—if their numbers continue to increase in the way they have over these first two years.

But back to the cloister garden, for my mind circles in wafts like the April breezes, as if some kind of whirlwind in the middle were to be avoided at all cost. In the center of the enclosed garden is the hawthorn we planted last September for the Feast of the Nativity of the Virgin before the frost set in. The branches boast sharp straight thorns with leaves deeply lobed, now newly green, promising both fragrant flowers and fruit for healing the heart. Mostly, though, I prize the tree as the axle for the knot-shaped herb garden; sweet and straight with its deep pink flowers already budded out, the center from which the planting of reviving perennials can be measured, and this year's new annuals can be seeded in rows that radiate out from it like the spokes in a wheel. It is our own sweet paradox: the thorn among what will be roses.

And so the thorn is at the center again, like the fixed thought of Rikkarda pricking at me. She above all would joy in this movement towards fruition, so like a druid herself in her knowledge of petals and plantings hand-pollinated for rich colors to lure the love of bees, combined for best-flavored honeys, from the dusky-dark buckwheats to light amber mint- and thyme-fed. Who now has the power to bring her back? If it is pride that is goading me, eating me away, let God in heaven punish me. My letter to her is nearly finished—too sensitive for dictation to Volmar or for the ears of any other scribe. I will finish it myself, be done with it, copy and dispatch it before Vespers.... "Woe is me, your mother, woe is me, daughter—why have you abandoned me like an orphan? I loved the nobility of your conduct, your wisdom and chastity, your soul and the whole of your life, so much that many said: What are you doing? Now let all who have a sorrow like my sorrow mourn with me—all who have ever, in the love of God, had such high love in heart and mind for a human being as I for you—for one snatched away from them in a single moment, as you were from me. But may the angel of God precede you, and the Son of God protect you, and His Mother guard you. Be mindful of your poor mother Hildegard, that your happiness may not fail."[100]

April 20, 1152
Third Sunday after Easter

 A courier appears from Aachen with the news that my letter to Frederick, now king of Germany, was received in time for his crowning on

[100]. Trans. Dronke, *WWMA*, pp. 156–57. Note that two themes dominate this portion of Hildegard's letter. One is the nearly Biblical quotation of the Lamentations of Jeremiah she sang during the Triduum of Holy Week, which are in liturgy the very epitome of loss, betrayal, and mourning. The second is the abbess's passionate abandonment of caution in her love for Rikkarda, so much so that it prompted "many" to say, "What are you doing?" Hildegard expresses a remarkably similar exchange

March 9th.[101] Read aloud amidst all of the congratulatory flattery, the admonitory tone of the letter may have scorched the ears of the German court. My source, the living God, is the only one to be trusted: Let King Frederick be warned about the reality of the times and the state of the Church in his empire. Abuses fulfill temptations, and there is no corner of the realm that is clean. Look how the growing diocese of Bremen is stuffed with a whole succession of newly created positions, and those filled with men and women lacking the proper age or experience to exercise their duties. Adelheid, too young even to have taken vows with us, and she's named and placed as abbess at Gandersheim![102] Consider that our own archbishop, Henry of Mainz, wrote to tell me that escorts sent to accompany Rikkarda to her new post at Bassum would be arriving here with his full knowledge and consent, and that I was to relinquish her without further opposition! Let it be known that he was warned about the sale of

through Ursula, who dares to voice her passionate yearning for Christ with the result that, "After Ursula had so spoken,/Popular opinion spread among all people everywhere./And the men said,/'The innocence of this ignorant girl!/She doesn't know what she's talking about!" (From "*O Ecclesia*" sequence, full text in Appendix.)

◼ 101. Hildegard corresponded with both Frederick Barbarossa (1152–90), crowned king in 1152 and Holy Roman Emperor in 1155, and with his predecessor King Conrad (1138–52), who had written asking specifically for her prayers for Frederick, his heir apparent. (Texts of letters in *PL*, pp. 185–87.)

◼ 102. Adelheid of Sommerschenberg, young niece of Rikkarda (daughter of Rikkarda's sister who by her third marriage became queen of Denmark), was briefly at Hildegard's convent, then called as abbess of Gandersheim while still an adolescent (at the same time that Rikkarda was called to the position at Bassum). (Flanagan, *Hildegard*, p. 180.) Only one of Hildegard's letters mentions her objection to the appointment, and there is no further mention of Adelheid, so we can presume that no further controversy ensued.

ecclesiastical offices in the reply I sent, that he was warned in addition about the fate of those who prevail against the will of God.[103] Not that he had ears to listen.

I wonder how it will go between us on the 1st of May. We will be obedient to his office. He comes officially to consecrate our unfinished church to the Mother of God and to his saints, Martin, Philip and James, and our patron saint, Rupert.[104] It is perfectly clear that the building cannot be completed in time—the painting is not half done—but in the Mass will be the new sequence for St. Rupert and the hymn for the Virgin. My pieces are inspired; they come from God, not from my own frail self, and they are ready to be sung. Let him have ears that hear this time. Let him see the curved wonder of the pelican breast of the baptismal font, the simplicity of the altar that houses the bones of our blessed Rupert, and the glowing colors that move in the compositions being painted on the wooden panels. Then let him take note of the beauty that exists in our church *in potentia*— a beauty that has grown from the inside out, so that when the painted depiction of the Heavenly Jerusalem is completed, he will see that it is a true symbol of what exists already in spirit today.

It isn't easy to flesh out a vision so clear on the inside, so hard to manifest in this world. Problems arise that I couldn't have imagined. The workmen piece together panels without consulting me, and I complain when it turns out badly. Of course each panel needs to be either entirely of larch or entirely of pine; to combine planks of the two kinds of wood within a single panel changes the colors of what is painted, and so in a pieced panel we end up with a botched, polyglot triptych instead of a single scene. Pegged and glued with infinite care, the colors still change dramatically when, for instance, two of the planks are of pine and one of larch. My master builder thinks to hide the fault by directing the painter to lay an extra coat of gesso on the surface before sketching, but it is still obvious to my eye.

It is why I have insisted on seeing each panel when the carpen-

103. See n. 73 above.

104. Newman, *Symphonia*, p. 295.

ters have done with their hatchets and checked their division of planks, and now I have set the painter with a three-foot mount for his easel in the cloister outside my own window for the good weather. My impatience outruns me, I know, but I will have both Ursula's journey and the Heavenly Jerusalem as perfect as they can be made. In a sense, the panels are born of me, and so my responsibility. They are like visual manifestations of the Ursula lyrics that have come to me; such paintings also bear unexpected fruit among some of my women. For the third day two young novices, with my permission, have spent their recreation period in rapt contemplation of the painting going on in the courtyard cloister. Yesterday my mistress of novices reported that she noticed some of the green earth used to paint the panels hidden in Christina's cell, her failure to ask permission making this a clear infraction of the Rule. She may yet have the courage to ask; I pray that she will. Verdigris makes for a brilliant green, so much better than the olive green from the buckthorn, and I am interested to see what kind of shape may emerge on the wall of her cell if she dares. Christina watches with great zeal; I have observed elsewhere that her hands and eyes work well together, and I feel she could be part of the seeding of our own scriptorium in time; illuminations bring a strong sense of life to manuscripts.

I myself have hoarded colors for years.... How else would we have the yellow orpiment for the auras that surround the heads of the holy or the exact ultramarine we need for the vast sea? The flowers begin to bloom in the newly raised beds outside the window, suggesting further colors, while those of my visions are still more varied. Of all of them, it is the gold that is hardest to come by: The powder is costly and scarce, and I would never dare to direct its use but for illuminations on vellum. There I will someday have it, because there is no other way to portray the radiance that both warms my physical body and sparkles behind my eyes.

I was delighting in colors when they rang the bell for me. A man had been brought from some

distance, probably having traveled through at least one night without food or rest. I don't know who looked more distraught and weary, the man himself or the woman whose hand he clutched. His eyes were intense and agitated, alternately darting in fear and then deeply melancholic. They were of a slate blue so deep as to seem gray-black. Here were colors of such complexity and carrying such a rich emotional content that my mind wandered for a moment to the selection of colors I had long been collecting for the purpose of illuminating visions, the colors I had reluctantly hidden away in a cupboard when the bell called me to the parlor.

An awful groan eructing from his belly through his throat shut out the other colors and pulled me, bent me to this agonized man and his eyes, with triangularly peaked flesh above the lids, like a pointed arch directly over the middle of each eye. The result was something nearly demonic about the eyes, and I knew then that there was likely a spiritual cause for the physical agony that coursed through him. About the woman, I could see nothing, because fear and what may have been a kind of grim determination held her face from free expression, but I sensed a particular strength in her, if only in the hand that he held; it looked as though her one tightly held hand was the single support for his much larger body, his head, and his peculiarly large hands.

His fingers were remarkably long, not tapered at the tip, but spatulate—a perfect hand for describing neumes,[105] it occurred to me. I wondered briefly whether he might be a can-

105. Written signs that remind the cantrix or cantor of the shapes to be made by the hand in the air while leading the choir in a piece of chant. In a 12th-century monastery, pieces were still learned by the choir as part of a long and complex oral tradition; cheironomy (the conducting of neumes) jogged the memories of the choir by indicating information about rhythm and about the rise and fall, the speed and contour of the melodic line.

tor; of course, if he were a monk, he would have gone to his own dispensary or confessor and not mine, not to speak of the puzzle of his female companion. A renegade monk perhaps, I was thinking, when another droning sigh interrupted. Quickly I raised my right hand to his upper spine between the two shoulder blades, my left to the front of his chest in the area of the sternum. Placed in this way, my hands were listening, although they barely touched the dark cloth of his shirt, and I was able to monitor the thudding movement and sounds that informed me that he was highly agitated and collapsed in upon himself at the same time.

The heartbeat was unusually loud, somewhat irregular, pausing briefly when the terror stormed through, then pushing on with accelerated force as if to overcome or deny what had so briefly but dramatically silenced and immobilized it. The notion of exorcism began to push at me, and immediately, words came to mind and began to fill me with their power. Then a strange thing happened: I noticed the man had grown much paler, was breathing in a shallow, over-excited manner, and that I had lost touch with all of the information I had been getting from my hands. I could practically see that wild and irregular heartbeat in the movement of his chest, but my hands picked up nothing. They were suddenly useless as sensitive instruments.

I must have given an involuntary groan of despair, which was immediately echoed by a much louder groan from him; his breathing became deeper, and I realized that it was I who had disrupted both of our breathing patterns. In my zeal for routing out the Devil, in my excitement to open the way for God's righteousness to enter, and caught up in my own concern for seizing the most powerful words I could find, I was hardly breathing at all, and this in turn curtailed his breathing and closed off all the rich communciation available through my hands. I couldn't help but laugh at myself, so busy routing out the Devil in him while I was getting all puffed up with pride. He laughed as well—out of relief, I suppose—and then began to talk.

It was the hero of Psalm 37 who now sat before me. It was there in everything he said:

I am become miserable
and am bowed down even to the end;
I walked sorrowful all the day long,
for my loins are filled with illusions
and there is no health in my flesh.
I am afflicted and humbled exceedingly;
I roared with the groaning of my heart. [106]

Unlike his groans and sighs, which were so loud, his words were low and terribly difficult to understand. His woman companion and I had to huddle around him in order to hear. I sat down on a stool; she, on the floor near his knees.

The bell.

 I learned on Friday that his name is   **May 11, 1152**
Basel, and he comes to us from the   **Sunday after Ascension**
splendid church of St. Gereon in
Cologne, where martyrs of the Theban legion are depicted in mosaics of such rich colors that I have heard people call them the Golden Saints.[107] He has prayed in the church of St. Ursula and is a living source of information about Cologne: its church architecture and liturgy, the ever-increasing number of heretics there known as Cathars, and also, of course, about music, because my observation about his hands was correct. He was cantor, although a secular priest and
not a monk; clerical, and not
monastic. Thus I can be sure
of the rifts that separate us, in
the ideal as well as the living
of our spiritual lives. It is also
true that the man has much
from which I could learn. He
has been librarian and scribe;

106. Vulgate Psalm 37:7–9.

107. Romanesque church dedicated to St. Gereon and his companions. These martyrs (whose numbers steadily increased as did those of Ursula's companions), mentioned in Bede's *Martyrology* and included in the Sarum calendar for October 10th, achieved great popularity in the 12th century, especially in Cologne.

his knowledge and skills are extremely broad. Of his depth, I can only surmise, for his mind is agitated, his soul disordered, his body therefore in a state of total exhaustion. Still, the eyes give evidence of great depth, which is verified by the wordless information my hands received on evaluating his heart, even through all the rough cloth on his back and his chest.

Meanwhile, the shiny, swollen joints in his feet tell of gout too painful for walking, and his disordered heart calls out for rest. As passionate as I feel, I will not begin by debating with him at this point about issues of clerical reform, and I would not refuse him help. The ringing of the bell cut us short before I could learn anything of his life on Ascension, the day he came, and on my way to Vespers I instructed my infirmarian to house him in the dispensary with as much privacy as is physically possible at present (he actually has a nice view of the growing structure of our cloister church), and to have his woman companion stay in the quarters with our lay sisters, at least until I can better assess their relationship as well as her character.[108] Today I learned from my feisty old Matilda that the companion, whose name is Agathe, is a skilled gardener and keeper of bees. She suffered urban confinement living within the city walls of Cologne, is excited by and intensely curious about our raised-bed system of gardening, and eager to help old Matilda. This is a blessing, now that crone, who is my best gardener, is propelled by little else besides pure spirit and vernacular curses, according to my daily observations.

On my way to singing Vespers that day, I acknowledged that my hope is in the living God, yes, but there are days when the terrors of decision making are particularly loud and God strangely quiet. Volmar is supportive of my

108. It is unlikely that the priest would have been married, because the prohibition against married clergy was accepted (following the reforms of Gregory VII) by this time; probably the woman was his concubine, which was neither an unusual arrangement, nor would it have been damaging to his clerical status, regardless of Hildegard's personal opinions about it.

decisions about Basel; still, I wonder at such a powerful intelligence and deep commitment gone astray. I wonder at some people being choked by ecclesiastical offices, others buying and selling them, the strain on the heart and the nerves. Singing Vespers, intoning the psalms for my women, observing the tolling bell after Compline, I wonder whether the psalms aren't my only consolation. Not just the sounds, but also the shapes of the cadences are so beautiful! Each ending differentiates itself in the way that it falls a little, then rises before its final descent, or perhaps climbs in gentle whorls and risings before finally falling. Each cadence is a way of framing the psalm-verse it surrounds, but it also bridges a psalm and its antiphon, which is itself another piece of a psalm, a fragment embedded in a melody that perfects it and makes it whole.

Not so with people and human events these days; my life becomes a series of interruptions, rather than nestling in the precious beads of the Divine Office that make up a necklace, the setting for the jewel of the Mass. The clamoring of outer events has grown louder than the *opus dei* and presents itself piecemeal: broken hearts and bones, spoiled meat, scorched altar cloths, exhaustion of medicines, withering spirits, the never-ending jealousies in the novitiate, and I suppose it was always the smooth touch of Rikkarda that sang them together for me. It is certainly not I, not the abbess on this Godforsaken mountain who has strung the beads smooth, unruffled the feathers, or stilled homesick sobs in the night.

It has been my lot to oppose the opposition, over and over again, win the scorched earth, battle for our autonomy, plot out the quarters and the cloister and the vineyards. To prescribe for each patient in the dispensary, set out the plan for the novitiate, interpret the Rule, choose the refectory readings, lead the offices with voice and hand, rouse them all to whatever learning they will have at all; only now do I realize that the care of their hearts was more hers than mine.

So I discover it was not just my own heart Rikkarda tended as my gray-eyed prioress, but all of our tender hearts which she soothed and wrapped and connected. But now what of hers? Now that she has strung all our hearts like delicate living pearls made of blood, of a loving pattern that pleases us all and makes our music more harmonious and my tender joints not so painful, is it her lot simply to move on, and to a foundation better endowed, much longer established? I wonder whether she ever really thought of our souls, of our spiritual selves at all. What feels like my soul was perhaps my heart all along. Could I have been betrayed by my own heart after so much suffering, such difficult years of growth, and so much attention to detachment from the more ordinary, obvious, clamoring temptations that buzz at me now as if they were truly my life? What a great failure that would be!

I go to Mass having heard my own confession.

 Much to my surprise, they came on the 1st bearing gifts. Archbishop Henry arrived at the gate with his   May 18, 1152   Feast of Pentecost

entourage, announced with alarm by my anxious portress, horses lathered and weary from the long, stony trek from Mainz. Almost as soon as perfunctory greetings were said, the bell rang for Prime. Let them be rubbed down, fed, and bedded in the carefully guarded remains of last year's sweet hay; they'll be more comfortable than we who have to face each other, sing to one another, and meet at the altar to be dedicated in space smelling of fresh paint and resins.

But thank God, the incense was there; incense can cover us all. The first gift was the genuine kindness and pleasure with which he received our offering, for we had used the prized sheet of vellum well: It was actually Volmar's suggestion that the sequence for St. Rupert be written out in careful text—that he himself would prepare it—with decorated initials at the words "O Jerusalem" at the first and last verses.[109] We intertwined them with acanthus leaves, with grape vines and braided knots, all colored with

  ▣ 109. Hildegard refers to the sequence she wrote for the patron saint of her church and community (*Lieder*, #37, pp. 91–97).

the fine powders the painter for the church has been using for the panels. On the creamy white skin the same colors glow even more like precious stones than on the darker wood panels.

A painting of the architecture of our cloister church was above the text; following that, the date of the dedication plus the name of Henry, the archbishop. At the end of our long sequence for St. Rupert, we added the text of the dedication hymn we favor, the *"Urbs beata ierusalem"*:

> *Jerusalem, blest city,*
>   *named "vision of peace,"*
> *Builded in the heavens*
>   *from living stones....*
> *By hammering and beating*
>   *your stones are polished*
> *And fitted to their places*
>   *by the Artist's hand,*
> *Laid in this everlasting*
>   *consecrated house.*[110]

Since it was done with such care and beauty, it seemed unlikely that he would disagree with its use in the *Ordo* we had prepared. Had he simply done what was required of him liturgically, it would have been enough; but he did more: He truly was observant of our progress in both building and planting, grateful for some degree of comfort in the lodgings we had prepared, and surprised at the glory of the sound that rose with the incense in the candled space where the choir sang—for it fanned and wafted out so, but with

110. Ancient (6th or 7th century) anonymous hymn written for the feast of the Dedication of a Church. Its opening lines celebrate the fact that in Hebrew the word "Jerusalem" means "vision of peace," and in the lines following we are introduced to the abiding tradition that speaks of the "living stones" as the souls of the faithful. (Cited by Newman in comparison with Hildegard's Sequence for St. Rupert in *Symphonia*, p. 295.)

such clarity as well, that when we ended with the recessional hymn "*O virga ac diadema*,"[111] dividing ourselves into two members that moved slowly down opposite aisles of the church, our alternations overlapped beautifully, the antiphonal pairing carrying across and echoing both heavenward and bouncing off all the angles of the walls.

His official gifts to us were three, like those of the Magi. The first was his signature with mine on a charter, an agreement about further land being granted directly to us, another step in our economic independence. The second was a small ring for an abbess, the kind that seals documents, carved ivory, delicate and simple in its beauty, the lone initial Ⱶ slightly retrocurved at the ends of the vertical strokes, like the petals of the freckled orange daylilies of our midsummer fields. The ring itself is of bronze, beaten and polished with a raised bezel in the center that holds the oval of carved ivory.[112] It could hang from my cincture. If I keep it on my hand, it is always ready for sealing the hot wax on letters and documents. But its own heat is noticeable if I rub it. It grows warm when I rub it, and it will stay on my hand.

The third gift was for

111. "O branch and crown of the King's royal purple/You, in your enclosure, are like a fortress." Opening of a sequence (used here as a recessional hymn) written by Hildegard for the Virgin Mary. Shortly after Hildegard's death, when the first attempt at canonization was made, several of her nuns testified that this was a favorite of Hildegard's and recalled the abbess pacing the cloister while humming "*O virga ac diadema*" and being illuminated from within by the Holy Spirit. (Full English text by author in *Signs*, V, 3, pp. 564–65.)

112. An abbess's ring, similar to the one described above, is part of the medieval collection at the Walters Art Gallery, Baltimore, MD. On the subject of adornment of Hildegard and her virgins, we have the letter of Tengswich, abbess of Andernach, who wrote asking Hildegard whether it was true, as she had heard, that on feast days Hildegard allowed her virgins to wear rings, white veils, and crowns bearing the image of the Lamb. Hildegard's long reply gives a forceful theological justification for such a practice, while never actually saying whether or

feeding through the eyes. The painting he brought was in keeping with the event we celebrated—a depiction of St. Augustine's City of God. In the painting, the City is well built and walled, bounded by tall towers, hung with banners of texts; the four evangelists have triple pairs of wings, each appearing in his proper iconographical aspect, so that Mark, Luke, and John are magnificent beasts. Busts of all the haloed, blessed ones stretch in slightly curving horizontal bands across the whole City, underlined with messages painted on scrolls. The Creator is enthroned on the rim of the orb; his feet rest on a parallel, lesser orb. The lamb of the Apocalypse is held in a lapis-filled circle in his right hand, the dove encircled the same way in his other hand, with a beautifully lettered scroll stretched between them. The figures of Wisdom and Jacob are prominent, one on either side of the golden aureole that surrounds the barefoot Creator. They also carry lettered scrolls. Like that city Augustine described, the painting is measured and perfect, ratios expressed, proportions figured, multitudes and triumphs contained. Nothing has been overlooked.

Looking at it now, I wonder how the perfection of such a painting so eludes my inner senses; I wonder if its containment deadens them, for I have feasted my eyes on it now each day of the weeks since it came. Its theme is so to my liking; more, to my heart and purpose here, the building and teaching, the order and measure of what must be accomplished; nevertheless, it is not what I experience in my gifts. It is not even the way I have learned what I know. It is not the way that my knowledge is acquired. It lacks the warmth of the bronze, the strong metal not the practice was hers. She points out that married women who are devout should follow the modesty requirements of I Timothy 2:9 insofar as they are identified with Eve and must obey their husbands. Professed virgins, on the contrary, are appropriately splendid in their perpetual, ever-renewing greenness (*viriditas*) and, like the virgins in the Book of the Apocalypse, are seemly when wearing on their person the image of the Lamb. Their modesty is sufficiently veiled by their virtue of humility (*PL*, pp. 336–38).

rounding my finger, rubbing to fiery flow in my hand. It streams not at all like the torrential fountains of fiery light that invaded my brain and whole being now ten years past. Tongues of Pentecostal fire burned into me, informing meanings and language: brilliant wings with eyes of God whipping the air to a frenzy of bright movement.

My frame is too frail to contain all this. I knew it to be physically true that I had been weakened further and further by illness, debilitated, having no strength for living in that place where I needed both to lead and to obey. But like the terrible burning bush of Moses this fire did not consume me; it branded me open, burned out any protection of innocence, melted my human resistance, emblazoned words clarion-clear, blown like horns of salvation, and poured them into my poor form the way a crucible is filled and brought to unbearable heat and, in breaking open, pours out its beauty like a molten river!

The power was not orderly or perfect, but too dangerously bright, nearly blinding the way it surrounded and carved out knowledge and images I couldn't have known, never had read, neither seen nor even heard from the lips of Jutta or Volmar. Totally inexplicable in the light of my human frailties and lack of education, but clear and energized, shaped by the heat of the finger of God.

✣ 113. Before the move to Rupertsberg, Hildegard had already set down the lyrics to fourteen liturgical pieces as part of the thirteenth vision of Book III of the *Scivias*, where they precede a first, sketchy version of the morality play *Ordo virtutum* (*PL*, pp. 729–38). The pieces are paired antiphons and responsories to be used at the Divine Office. Since only their texts appear in the *Scivias*, there is no definitive answer to the question of whether Hildegard composed the words and music at the same time; however, because of the repeated references to music in the texts of all of the visions in Book III, vision 13, my guess would be that these existed in both the music and words in a version that—like the *Ordo*—became musically elaborated for regular liturgical use and was eventually recorded in written notation during the early years at Rupertsberg, when Hildegard was able to exercise full autonomy

Many of the songs that I have composed we are now able to sing for the Divine

Office here; they are recorded in the *Scivias*,[113] but I hadn't really thought much about the possibility of writing down the melodies as well as the texts until yesterday, when, for the entire time between Prime and Terce, Basel, Volmar, and I discussed reasons for continuing to write things down now that the *Scivias* is completed. Basel suggested that I think about how carefully I keep our calendar and how indispensable it is to the life and liturgy of our community. He said that it is also a record of the particular way we celebrate here, the fact that we celebrate the feast of our blessed Rupert on May 15, for example, making us different from Benedictine communities in France and England. The music that we sing in praise of St. Ursula in October is unknown except to the singers. And notating the melodies and texts of my new songs on vellum would result in a permanent descriptive record of how we praise God in this convent. Volmar, of course, was in agreement.

When I then protested my ignorance of the rules of notation, Basel pointed out that the neumes are simply transcriptions of the hand signs that I always use as cantrix; that, just as Volmar has written down the words I dictate, so he could write down the over the musical practice of her entire community. A letter to Hildegard from Odo of Soissons written in 1148 (*PL*, p. 352) attests to the fact that some songs of hers (*modos novi carminis*) were known abroad even before she left Disibodenberg; however, the likelihood is that by *carminis* (songs) Odo refers to the texts—just as we say *hymns* when we really mean hymn *texts* set to traditional melodies. Hildegard's melodies were far from traditional, even those of her hymns, so it is possible that the melodies themselves were not known outside Hildegard's community before she sent them to the monks of Villers in the form of what is now known as Codex D (Codex 9 at the library of Pieters & Paulusabdij, in Dendermonde, Belgium), which was made c. 1175 at the scriptorium of St. Rupertsberg under Hildegard's supervision.

new songs that we sing, transcribing from my hand and voice, as it were. Using the manuscript that Basel had brought from Metz as an exemplar, Volmar was able to grasp the conventions of the process without difficulty.[114] He could even train one of my women to do the same, he suggested, and she could then be responsible for being my musical scribe. It is not for teaching the songs, which must always be through the body—from my inner ears and hand to their outer eyes and ears—but for describing our practice here, ensuring its consistency, and aiding my memory as cantrix. It could help my women begin to think of themselves as members of a Benedictine community that exists at a particular place and time, and for a reason we may not yet fully comprehend. I think of it as an awareness of our particular role in the history of salvation.

It is an intriguing suggestion; of course, Basel could not know to what extent the "writing down" of things has already plagued me: the Voice of Wisdom that exhorts me to write things down has been with me for such a long time now, and, for the many years that I ignored her, I suffered horribly in my body, for in that sense the "body is the garment of the soul."[115] When Pope Eugenius, at the Synod of

114. Late in her life, Hildegard was quoted as saying that she brought forth and sang chant with music in praise of God and the saints without the instruction of anyone, and sang although she had never learned either musical notation or singing (*PL*, p. 104). When she says this, it is more than saying she has not been to a school, because what was taught in school was called *musica*, not *cantus*, and was theoretical (theorems of Pythagoras, ratios, modes, music of the spheres, its relationship to geometry and arithmetic) rather than the practical matter of singing the corpus of Mass and Divine Office chants; these were taught by the cantrix and prioress, or novice mistress, in the novitiate of the convent. Hildegard is protesting that she didn't even have that kind of formal training—which makes the exercise of her musical gifts all the more remarkable.

115. Hildegard uses versions of this thought in many contexts; for example, in her letter to the prelates of Mainz, she says, "The body is truly the garment of the soul, which has a living

Trier, identified my gift as the charism of prophecy, and encouraged me to continue the setting down of my visions, the illnesses that had intensified prior to beginning the formal recording of *Scivias* were largely assuaged. During the years preceding, as I suffered physical torments, I thought often about all the power-filled prophets of the Old Testament, like Ezekiel and Jeremiah, who saw so deeply into the divine mysteries. These were men powerfully gifted to see, even to speak, but they were not instructed to write down what they saw. During those years at Disibodenberg, whenever liturgical lessons at Matins or Mass were from the prophetic books, I would listen with greatest care and meditate upon them in my mind, hoping that, the more I understood about the Old Testament prophets, the better the possibility for me to understand and be obedient to my own gift.

Jonah was also reluctant to do what he seemed chosen to do. He was stubborn in his body, and, again and again, his own willful pride attempted to interfere with God's plan for him. But for Jonah not to interfere with God's plan was simply to be. For Jeremiah not to interfere with God's plan was simply to bear witness to the wrongs his people did all around him, to understand how they were rejecting God Himself, betraying His love for them. Jeremiah needed simply to stand in the marketplace and express his sorrow, to open his mouth so that God's anguish and misery with His treacherous people could be heard. It was different for me, and I was still in doubt about the particular demands for writing things down that God placed on me through the Voice of Wisdom. For one thing, as a woman I had never received formal training in grammar and rhetoric, and was not in the habit of writing things down; furthermore, as a woman I was expressly forbidden to teach publicly, even if my visions and prophecies were a gift from God.[116]

voice; for that reason it is fitting that the body simultaneously with the soul repeatedly sing praises to God through the voice." (*PL*, p. 221.)

116. Hildegard explained the first handicap in an autobiographical fragment of her *Vita* (*PL*, pp. 383–84). The stricture against any woman

Nevertheless I persisted, and it was my deep understanding of two prophetic books—the Book of the Apocalypse and my most beloved Book of Psalms—that led me to begin dictating my visions to Volmar. In the Book of the Apocalypse appears the woman clothed in the sun, whose particular shape and glory we revere in the liturgical texts on August 15th, for the Feast of the Assumption of the Virgin. She is especially beloved to me because of the particular quality of radiance she bears, so like the light that emanates from my visions of the figures of Ecclesia, Caritas, Sapientia, and the Virgin Mother of God. In the Apocalypse, she is crowned with stars, with the moon under her feet, and it is the earth that saves her from the forces of evil that threaten her own life and that of the child she bears.[117] I began to understand a relationship between these numinous women who appeared to me transfigured—so illuminated from within by a divine radiance that filled them and extended outwards all around as if wrapping them in the very light they had emanated—and the remarkable woman in the Apocalypse. I began to pay more attention to the words and the form of the Apocalypse of John the Evangelist.[118] The scrolls, I thought, the scrolls: here is a prophet who is told he must write what he sees, no matter how strange teaching outside of her own home—promulgated since the early days of the official practice of the Church—was finally codified in great detail by Thomas Aquinas in his *Summa theologica*. According to Aquinas, even if the woman was recognized officially as having received the gift of prophecy (as was the case with Hildegard), she should in all cases, like Mary, keep the prophecy close to her heart and in silence.

117. "The serpent poured water like a river out of his mouth after the woman, to sweep her away with the flood. But the earth came to the help of the woman, and the earth opened its mouth and swallowed the river which the dragon had poured from his mouth." (Apoc. 12:15–17.)

118. For Hildegard, both John's Gospel and the Book of the Apocalypse were written by the same disciple.

119. Various commentators have noted this

it may sound; over and over again it is the scrolls that are evoked to reveal these mystical texts, so that we understand their mysterious cadences as being read and sung, not simply spoken.[119] We have these visions because St. John did what he was ordered. Something about the writing slipped into place for me, and the possibility that it was not humility, but pride, that was keeping me from writing presented itself as well.

After that, I began to realize that the 150 psalms in the Divine Office we pray each week of the year in fact make up a single book, a prophetic book, and that these prophecies are also and have always been embodied as songs. Dearer to me than almost anything I know, my greatest comforters, God's highest praises and thanksgivings: The psalms are prophetic, they are songs, and they are a book! In this way it seemed possible, according to what I knew, to embody my own prophetic gift in songs and words, and I zealously began to obey the voice of Sapientia by recording what I saw and heard in the book of visions that came to be called *Scivias*. What still hadn't occurred to me before Basel's suggestion of yesterday was to record the shapes of the melodies themselves, not only the words. I feel this might help me to stabilize the ever-increasing variations of music I must organize and teach for the performance of the play of the sixteen Virtues and their queen.

difference, as well as the approbation of charismatic ministry in the Apocalypse, which surely supported Hildegard's decision to be heard. For example, "In St. Paul's time the utterances and exhortations of the prophets were wholly oral. Later, in the *Apocalypse*, prophecy under the new covenant takes a written form. Both the prologue and the epilogue claim that the *Apocalypse* is a prophecy and the prophet has brother-prophets (22:9). The Church, as viewed in the *Apocalypse,* is Spirit and Bride, the charismatic ministry and a body of believers. No special place is assigned to bishops, priests, deacons—unless they were also prophets, as may sometimes have happened. We read of 'prophets and saints,' [of] 'saints, apostles, and prophets.' Unlike St. Paul, the Apocalyptist's view of the Christian ministry is wholly charismatic and

The light is delicious. We were able to have a long practice between Vespers

and Compline to learn the music for the Vigil of St. John the Baptist. Now a melon-colored light still remains and will continue long enough for me to observe the turn-around-the-poles of the summer solstice as I write to young Elisabeth of Schönau.[120] News has come that she was deathly ill for several weeks beginning at Pentecost, and I am not surprised, considering the anguish she has expressed to me, with her extreme fear of criticism. Even though I cannot break the Great Silence to dictate to Volmar at this hour, she must hear from me; he can make a fair copy in the morning. ‡‡ *Listen, then, my troubled daughter: The whispering of the ambitious serpent sometimes seeks to wear down precisely those people our God instructed through divine inspiration. For when the old snake spots a gem of special worth, he hisses, raising himself up, and says: "What is that?" And then he torments with many afflictions the heart that longs to fly above the clouds (as the old serpent himself once did), as though human beings were gods.*

And now I want you to listen further to me. Those who long to bring God's words to completion must always remember that, because they are

prophets are held in high esteem.... It is usually thought that prophecy as an institution or element inherent in the life and worship of the Church suffered an eclipse in the second century." (Potter in Aquinas, *Summa*, vol. 45, p. 159.)

■ 120. Elisabeth of Schönau (1129–65), German Benedictine nun thirty years younger than Hildegard, began writing letters to the abbess in the 1150s, asking for encouragement for her life and writing. Although St. Ursula's name is never mentioned in any of the correspondence, in fact Elisabeth was at this same time producing a series of fantastic visions about Ursula & the 11,000 Virgins, which included recordings of lengthy conversations with Cordula, a follower of Ursula who had initially escaped the martyrdom. Elisabeth dictated these visions to her brother Egbert beginning in 1156. The dating, plus the enormous difference in content and artistic depth, makes it unlikely that Hildegard's lyrics were in any way dependent

human, they are vessels of clay and so should continually focus on what they are and what they will be. They should leave heavenly things to the One who is heavenly, for they are themselves exiles who do not recognize what is heavenly. They only announce the mysteries like a trumpet, which indeed allows the sound but is not itself the source that produces the note. For someone else is blowing into the trumpet and causing the note to be produced.

They should put on the armor of faith, being mild, gentle, poor, and despised. This was the condition of that Lamb whose trumpet notes sound in them from the childlike intuition of their behavior. But God always disciplines those who blow God's trumpets, and God sees to it that the earthen vessel does not break, but pleases the Divine.[121] ‡‡

How well I remember as a young nun the torment of keeping silence for all of those years, and until I was much older than Elisabeth is now. The intensity of what I saw and heard made it even more frightening; the clarity sometimes led me to suspect that people around me could see what I was witnessing, and their derision was therefore more devastating.

One of the few things I recall from the days before St. Disibode's, as a very small child, is that peculiar quality of light one Midsummer Eve in which I began to see with my inner senses; first, the figures were in silhouette, the way they look in the west as the sun sets and shapes of trees or a single twisted branch make dark calligraphs that seem to come forward. It took months before the light really filled the figures and brought them to life, colors gradually permeating the shapes as they began to assemble themselves into larger figures, recognizable physiognomies, whole landscapes. But one day, there it was, bright and wordless, a mysterious, silent world so different from the commerce, the business of my father's house, the bustle of those in attendance, the cries and arguments and play of my sisters and brothers who were all older and more able, somehow more vig-

upon those of Elisabeth, which were called "The Book of Revelations of Elisabeth, of the sacred band of the virgins of Cologne."

■ 121. Trans. Miller in *HvB's Bk. of Divine Works*, pp. 339–40.

orous, more familiar with one another and with what the world would require of them.

Perhaps it was the succession of plants that began to give me some sense of a design that included me, plants whose colors and fragrances so suffused my senses that I could carry them with me, pull them into my soul where they could be mysteriously watered by the fountain of the Father and begin to inform me of other ways of knowing. Starting in earliest spring, the first blossoms I found were low and hidden, pungent and musky smelling, darkly colored, carpeting the banks of brooks and spreading gradually from lowlands through a whole spectrum of colors until—at midsummer—the yellows of helianthus and solidago blazed with the fuchsia of wild phlox while the vermilion of bergamot was like molten fire.

I remember gathering leaves, petals, and whole flower heads in my small, sticky hands, palming their silky surfaces until they had given up all their oily fragrances into the skin of my hands. Finally, when they became papery, I would put collections of them under my light summer quilt. But some of the smells always remained, or mysteriously returned, and it was like sleeping in a fragrant meadow; after a while I could even carry the secret fragrance with me into the clear light of day. More and more I learned the way to coax myself into the inner world, all the while believing that this silent experience was common to the development of all children. For it somehow seemed safe to see the strange pictures of my inner landscape while resting in such a fragrant meadow.

 Matilda is the first of us to die here, and that entirely without warning, unshriven, sprawled

June 24, 1152

Nativity of John the Baptist

among knots and curves of the garden of medicinals and herbs she had tended, nursed, and brooded over since our move to this mount of blessed Rupert.

During all my years at St. Disibode's, the only professed woman to die in our community was my old teacher Jutta. Most of the rest are so much younger, so full of health and tenacity and the kind of worldly vanity that gives tremendous vitality when snared by the Holy Spirit: It is what I secretly love to see in my raw novices, what provides substance for the formative Rule to which we all yield.

What a difference in these two deaths—the shock of Matilda against that of Jutta so worn, my mother in spirit and in learning, my first experience of cantrix, of wise healer, gentle keeper! With all that, I know her way was never quite at home in community. Her growing life had ripened her as an anchoress; much as she cared for me and mothered me well, even as a youngster when it was only the two of us, I was never unmindful that my entrance into her life, the responsibility she acquired with my care, would not have been her choice. "Not my will but Thine" took on a poignancy and personal meaning for me because of Jutta, for I knew how dearly she had won her solitude and what a strange twist it was that, with the advent of my care and my own subsequent maturing vocation, our small female community would inevitably grow, in spite of that abbess whose heart longed for nothing but God and pure ether.

Everything seemed to intrude on poor Jutta, and it was a large part of my job as her protégé, and later as prioress, to protect her from sounds of giddy girls, suffering penitents, and even warbling birds.

So it came to be that her long, slow suffering approach to death afforded her the solitude she so desired. It must have been during those long months that I began to understand our enormous differences, and to wonder at them. I became more and more conscious of how carefully and precisely I could carry on my outer life—and not with any disconnection from the spiritual life—while allowing my inner ears and eyes to remain wide open. I could be a kind of sieve like the pelican's mouth, so that any contemplative wonder, picture, or mystery might breeze by in the Shadow of the Living Light, be caught, be turned like a many-faceted prism, sing or shine its hidden nature, even as I was teaching a lesson, praying the Psalter, or even pleading a case.

In fact, this became a particular blessing when I was nursing the sick those many years of my healing apprenticeship in the dispensary at Disibodenberg, and it is what sustained me through Jutta's long dying. Had I not recognized this way of using both inner and outer senses simultaneously, I could not have arrived here in this strange new land, nor survived these first two years at all intact. Furthermore, had my old Jutta been able to develop this kind of constructive duality, I am convinced her life could have been longer and her death less of an agony. As it turned out, her concentration was so extremely delicate that any unwonted stimuli, whether inner or outer, interrupted her prayers and disrupted her contemplative life. Physical pains, even twinges or rumblings from her weakening gut, were rending interruptions, as were any sounds of the ordinary day's chores and constructions, and her last days were a torment from trying to focus. Bits of oiled milkweed silk I daily prepared and warmed in my praying hands to put into her ears each morning as the day's sounds began, and then more medicinals and even narcotics I prepared to dull and still her as far as I dared.

Towards the end, her torment was so great, her energy so dissipated and her attention so impossible to focus, that I would elevate her upper body where she lay, then climb onto the bed behind and under, straddling my legs beneath her withered pelvis. Then I would breathe audibly, coaxing her breathing into a more monotonous regularity with my breathing, in tune with my body, so that, when we began to sing, we could be as one and her spirit finally could be free in its solitary search after God. Still, it was a difficult going-out for Jutta. At the end, her room had to remain dark at all times, and my tending her was clumsy with fumbling and stumbling in the shadows. There was some way in which her faith was failing her, and her reasoning mind scrambled to prepare for what she could neither envision nor trust. And so the darkness, as if to force herself into submission for the worst she could imagine. This wonderful woman who had guided me in observing the range of positions of the rising and setting sun, who had had me mark with a crayon on a wall the time and place where the warming sunlight first appeared in the morning and finally disappeared each and every day of my eleventh year, ended by begging me to bind her eyes to the already dim shadows in her one-windowed dying room.

And now this sudden death of Matilda, at a midday, fragrant herb stalks still pressed in one leathery hand; bright death splayed amidst the roses and beetles; aphids and buzzing bees mingling around the wreath she had on her head in late June. Clogs on her calloused, blackened feet, this short, sturdy lay sister who joined us at age fifty-eight, mother of seventeen children, eleven living and troublesome, all from one mean buzzard of a husband, his death attested to by friends and relatives, he no doubt foraging yet across the Rhine in someone's fields for food, shelter, and a tired woman to bed him again. But Matilda was ours for eight years. She almost single-handedly transplanted what she could ransack with impunity from Disibodenberg's gardens, and also started anew herbs, flowers, and simples for our table, resurrected the orchard that gives shape and fragrance to our cemetery, all this with joy and curses regularly howling at the elements. Dear my God, we are blessed in the death of such passionate life!

 Hours after Compline, the sky still held the light; the feverishness began once

July 22, 1152, Midsummer Eve
Feast of St. Mary Magdalene

again in my feet. It is not only the burning sensation, but the toes and soles actually change color as if the blood and air fan each other, and so deepen the skin. Walked briskly in the cloister to disperse the burning as well as the thoughts that come almost nightly now to plague me about Rikkarda. Could I have done more to prevent her leaving? Did she actually seek out the appointment, never telling me in order to spare my all-too-human feelings? Sweet woodruff in sprightly clumps strews itself between the stones that delineate paths in the herb garden here, guiding my poor feet with its apple-green, the perilously sharp-thorned hawthorn begins to show its heart-easing berries now that the blooms have gone, and my agitated state begins to be eased as well.

The long row of linden trees, like rooted clouds, is even more pungent in the evening air than by day, and we have already begun the drying of its blossoms, enough to guarantee its fragrant tea over the length of the winter. It is time now to train the quince tree against the south wall of the building, letting it configure the outstretched arms of the crucified, of the cross itself: such drastic training of branches, pruning to one recognizable, austere shape so ruthlessly effective in focusing its vital growth. The day warmth of the late July sun has soaked into the cloister wall; as I search for the outline the espaliered quince will take, its rough warmth livens the tips of my fingers, soaks into my palm. Evening prepares for the very late rising of the full midsummer moon with a glow almost like dawn haloing the trees on the mountainous horizon, and in a quick moment a woman emerges from the warm wall, not silhouetted by the setting sun, but bathed and dripping with light. She is *mulier amicta sole*, clothed with the sun, the moon and stars under her feet, her head crowned as befits our woman of Psalm 45 with whom we sing, "Hearken, daughter, and incline thy ear, for the King greatly desires you."[122] And my own frail frame feels chosen and radiant, the music begins to move itself through my chest and ears, and she is moving her hand to the shape of a new song. It is not really separate neume-shapes she describes, though her fine hand moves, palm down, fingers together and slightly angled at the large

122. This text, and other verses of Vulgate Psalm 44, plus choral texts borrowed from the Propers of some of the Church's earliest venerated virgins, such as Agnes and Agatha, are the substance of offices for the Common of Virgins that gradually emerged as a separate section in monastic choral books during the medieval period. (The grouping of texts for the various feasts of the Virgin Mary is a clear example of this historical development; its eventual result was a *Common* for all Marian feasts, which was used in combination with several particular texts uniquely proper to her Birth [September 8], Purification [February 2], Annunciation [March 25], and Assumption [August 15], the four Marian feasts universally in place in Western Christendom by the 12th century.)

knuckle just like a *tractulus*, the inverse of our darting barn swallows in flight; rather, it is her whole arm, arched at the elbow, inscribing arcs and ellipses and then complete circles growing larger and larger as they finally stream from the radiant arched arm itself into curved ribbons of light across the whole sky. The music is strong and wave-shaped, slowly climbing in rounded turnings to surround the reciting tone where it hovers and undulates. It fills my inner ears like the rush of a waterfall, and I see the virgin faces, familiar, encircling me like a collar on the choir of angels: they, my builders in the dawn, my lovely artisans of Jerusalem, reflecting Christ the King. They are the living stones of the City, first earth-colored, then coloring to lapis, topaz, and emerald green, burning into the angles and facets of jewels, yet again transforming into the garden of blossoms and finally ebbing away in a long drawn-out sigh, the sound itself exuding the odor of flowers:

> *O you beautiful faces,*
> *Beholding God and building in the dawn,*
> *How noble you are*
> *In whom the King reflected Himself*
> *When He showed forth in you all the heavenly jewels;*
> *And as you are also redolent with all those jewels*
> *You are also the sweetest garden.*[123]

 These "monk-priests"! I hear they "say" their Masses, some in separate chapels, eliminating the singing of Ordinaries that rightfully belong to the people as well as of the choral Propers, the beloved province of *schola* or choir. No need for Introits, when no one enters—least of all Christ the King! No need for Offertories with their winged, cantorial

July 27, 1152
Tenth Sunday after Pentecost

⊡ 123. This antiphon is clearly written for Hildegard's own virgins, condensing some of her most cherished beliefs about their sacred role as builders of the Heavenly Jerusalem.

verses, when no one brings gifts, neither the local community nor the larger community they might serve. New books are produced, but in the service of whom? What they are calling *Missale* contains all the choral Propers (to be mumbled), the collects and readings for every day, no longer observing the injunction of Christ Himself that the thanksgiving banquet be celebrated where and when two or three faithful are gathered, ignoring the rule of Psalm 150 that always and forever we need to be praising Him in song.

The Dragon must be delighted at such developments, full of himself, swishing his tail at such observances. The elimination of music in praise of God can be the work of none other. The "saying" of Mass to benefit some individual soul has no place in the life of either the cathedral clergy or the monastic community. Basel tells me as well of books called *Breviarium*, whose use began as a convenience for monks who were traveling from their houses on various missions; now breviaries are produced in ever greater number, encouraging private recitation of the Office, just as missals do for the Mass. So even the Divine Office falls prey to such abuses. I understand from Basel they must now build their monastic churches with such practices in mind—with small, private chapels, hidden sanctuaries off the nave and transepts where individual monk-priests can whisper their individual prayers and offices, where individual priests can minister to no one but themselves, perhaps receiving money as well for a Mass in memory of one who needs indulgences to atone for the sins of this life.[124]

It is against such odds that Basel returns to Cologne, to his former post as cantor at St. Gereon's, for of course there are yet important feasts and celebrations for which his services remain useful. Some of the clergy there still remain faithful to sung offices, and music must be taught and sung for those who continue to minister to the people of his congregation when they celebrate the Eucharist. Not that I wasn't myself somewhat taken aback to discover that Basel was leaving today. A message through Volmar indeed! giving thanks for our nursing him back to health and, having been called back to St. Gereon's with impunity, wishing us well in all of our musical endeavors! And Basel having just begun to take down the music of my Play of the Virtues. Had I been given the opportunity to remonstrate, he would probably have assured me that Volmar—soon Sr. Radegund as well—can carry on the task of notation with competence. So be it.

By the time of our next Advent-Epiphany Season, the *Ordo virtutum* can be performed in our cloister church, even if it takes many more months before either the church or the Play of the Virtues is completed. No private chapels here. That is why, in planning the church, the openness was crucial, the inclusiveness, the nobility of a place of beauty where people can worship and learn. We might have been a Roman basilica, a large house in Jerusalem, but always warm and open, with ratios that carry sound in its own proportions. Bernard's Cistercians insist upon ascetic plainness in spaces of worship, that they be clear and without any color or adornment; indeed, Bernard presses this argument in theological texts of such elaborately beautiful prose that they themselves become flowers of persuasion. But since I grew up with the ideals of Cluny transplanted to the wilds of Disibodenberg, colors and curves are almost a part of the nature of community praise for me.

Still, so much of that beauty was denied to us for so long, so much left to our young imagining.[125] Tucked into the wall for most of the day at the very beginning, when Jutta was still housed as a hermitess, and later, singing our offices not in the large church with the rest of the monastic community, who were monks, but in the small Lady

124. Hildegard, in all of her complaints that open this particular entry, reminds us of the root meaning of the word "liturgy," from the Greek meaning "act of the people." Whether liturgy is used to refer specifically to the Eucharist, as the chief act of public worship, or in a larger sense to designate the prescribed canonical or monastic hours as well, liturgy is specifically in contrast to private devotion. St. Benedict made it clear in his Rule that he intended the Divine Office to be sung in community.

125. Disibodenberg, a monastery founded in the 8th century by Irish monks, was Hildegard's

Chapel where visitors and common townspeople gathered, we heard our voices as lonely animal sounds in that space, unsure of the psalm tones and cadences, especially when it was, at the first, just Jutta and I. The joy of having the number of women grow so that the sound could be raised! And finally, our housing space was clearly not large enough, as more and more of us gathered and our singing space needed to be separate from those visiting worshippers.

Our own church at St. Rupertsburg will hold all of us, as well as the visitors from Bingen. The formal dedication is behind us now, but more seems required to make it our own. By October we will have learned all of the new music for both Mass and Office to celebrate St. Ursula's feast day; in December or January we will do the *Ordo virtutum*. The singing of the Virtues will carry beautifully within these walls and set a tone congruent with the particular ideals of this female community. My visions are persistently filled with the Virtues of late. They come in their characteristic colors, moving in their prophetic, emblematic trappings. The first fruits of this vision appeared as words in the *Scivias*, but they grow with their music like a burgeoning garden in my mind

home for forty years. It was completely destroyed in the 18th century, although carefully planned archeological excavation has recently been undertaken. The results of this study and rebuilding promise to add to our knowledge of the housing of Hildegard and Jutta and of the small women's community that developed there. Many questions remain, but it seems certain from records that during Hildegard's lifetime the large monastic church at Disibodenberg (claimed to be almost as large as Mainz Cathedral) was built. It is unlikely that men and women sang the Divine Office together, even though some Hildegard scholars now refer to Disibodenberg as a "double monastery." A visit to the site in 1987, at the very beginning of its excavation and including complete projected architectural renderings, made a lasting impression on me and suggested as many historical questions as solutions. For further information about the rebuilding of Disibodenberg, there is now a foundation, needful of contributions, and willing to send literature, which may be contacted through Scivias-Stiftung, 6559 Odernheim, Germany.

now that we are settled in our own home. Indeed, just in the last week, something about having seen some of it on the page immediately suggests further varieties and expansions of the melodies.

We wish for Basel a safe return to Cologne.

 First they rule the vellum with scribing tools, paint the line for *ut* [do] in yellow and the one for *fa* in red; neumes that represent the cheironomic gestures are then superimposed on the whole structure of four lines and three spaces, so there is no mistaking the distance one is required to travel in the hexachord when singing through that phrase of the text.[126] No longer is this simply a general description or reminder. But suppose, the next time we sing this song, that the music coming through my body and into my cheironomic hand describes something slightly different; which is correct, the movement of my hand, or the neumes on the vellum? And while the pitches are precisely indicated, the rhythm of the words and the movement of the spiritual line—especially at melis-

August 3, 1152
Eleventh Sunday after Pentecost

⬛ 126. The great medieval music theorist Guido d'Arezzo (990–1050) designated the initial syllables of the first six lines of a hymn to St. John the Baptist as the names for the six notes of the hexachord: "*Ut* quant laxis/*Re*sonare fibris/*Mi*ra gestorum/*Fa*muli tuorum/*Sol*ve polluti/*La*bii reatum,/Sancte Johannes. [That with easy voices thy servants may be able to sing the wonders of thy deeds, remove the sin from their polluted lips, O holy John.] The first tone of each phrase of the melody moves in ascending order of tone, tone, tone, semitone, tone to designate the progression of each hexachord and could be represented by a particular progression on the digits of the hand. The system was capable of accommodating all eight of the church modes, and, if the range of a melody was extensive, two or three hexachords might be required, interlocked by a process called mutation. As a memory aid these tones and hexachords were pictured on diagrammatic hands (*manus musicalis*) seen in many medieval and Renaissance music treatises.

mas[127]—are less clear with the incised lines and prescribed neumes. Nevertheless, it gives a visual dimenion that was before totally lacking.

As melodies for the *Ordo virtutum* are notated, and the neumes spin in and around—and sometimes over and above—the four scribed lines, I see in a new way the ugliness of the Devil, for whom I have composed no music. Now I see his words all bunched together, crammed into a dense pocket of evil, lacking entirely the sense of movement and space that allows the songs of the women to breathe and dance on those lines, and only now do I understand why he has none: For all of these weeks that the songs of Castitas [Chastity], Contemptus mundi [Scorn for the World],[128] Discretio [Discretion], or Humilitas [Humility] (there are now sixteen female Virtues plus the queen) have been singing in my inner ear, it never occurred to me that the reason I heard no music for the Devil was because it is the Devil's job to silence music.

He refuses to acknowledge the power of music, just as he doesn't really see the women, or recognize the strength of their virtues. This is a vision that came to me several years ago, with the last of the *Scivias* material, in words and images I barely understood at the time. For performance in our own cloister church, the Virtues I have created will add their own voices, each have her own music, be incarnate. If the body is truly the garment of the soul, these virtuous souls will move in the bodies of my (not so virtuous) women. They clamor for the gowns and colors this affords, and it is a way for them to understand the inner activity of good and evil when they are lifted into the light. The

127. In contradistinction to syllabic passages of chant, where a syllable is sung to one to four tones of the melody, melismas are those musical phrases or clauses—often highly florid and improvisatory in nature—sung on a single vowel sound, with no change of textual underlay. This makes them much more difficult to fix in the memory.

128. "I pray not for the world," Christ said to His disciples (John 17:9). In light of His rejection, Hildegard held that scorn for, and even defiance of, the world's values and abuses was an important virtue for monastics.

Virtues arrange and rearrange themselves to my inner senses in a way that is never profane, and the fools who oppose it fail to see that, far from being a worldly show of activity, it is precisely the fruit of my contemplative life incarnate.

Nor am I presuming to create new liturgy, which is fixed for all time, and was made eternal by its consecration.[129] When we eat the Body and drink the Blood, it is the anamnesis in which we truly participate. We enter the eternal moment: It is always the same, though we ourselves age, wither, grow sick, recover, or grow thin, fat, wise, or foolish. Our participation in this eternal present is constant in the Eucharist: singing the prescribed choral Propers and leading the people in Ordinary sections of the Mass.

Our paricular work is the singing of offices by day and by night. In this continual work, our participation in the Divine Office, we have both more variety and more autonomy than in the Mass. We are not dependent upon priests, and we engage in every variety of prayer and thanksgiving, listening and learning, honoring and bearing witness not only to Christ and the Holy Mother of God, but to all the saints and doctors, wise teachers and holy women in the historical life of our Church. Liturgical time is sacred time, but dependent for its being and perpetuation on the re-creative, dedicated life of our community. The order of the sacred hours, the calendar of saints, the particular psalms for each office are fixed by a canon of laws and the Rule of St. Benedict. By our faithful observance of the Rule, we in a sense become life-givers to this sacred history of the Church on earth.

But there are still other ways that we as holy virgins can ourselves participate in this ongoing history. As exemplars, we have women from the very earliest days, starting with the three Marys at the tomb.

129. The liturgy in the Western Church was largely unchanged from the Carolingian era to Vatican Council II. The antiphons, responsories, hymns, and sequences written by Hildegard, as the tropes or textual/musical additions of the 10th–12th centuries, were meant to embellish what was already "given."

The *Quem queritis* antiphon [Whom do you seek?] that we sing in the Easter Matins Nocturn proclaims an extraordinary faith, and it is fitting and just that the three flesh out the original dialogue among themselves as they fan the Spirit that hovers around and through them.[130]

In the Order of the Virtues that has appeared to me, the Virtues are not Biblical women like the three blessed Marys, nor do they have their origin among the company of saints or holy women of history. They are creatures whom we will animate, whose reality becomes clear only as they acquire the capacity for thought and reason, movement and sound. All prayer is heightened in music, and so their words become elevated in the eyes of God. Volmar continually warns that the prelates of Mainz will ask about my sources, but it is of course God, through me, as the merest feather on His breath.[131] I wonder how they will greet the gowns! His Holiness at Rome moves about his Holy See to various stations in his finest garb. He moves with all of his clergy and his *schola cantorum* to stations at Maria Maggiore and St. John Lateran; they process in their finest, believing that nothing less can appropriately honor the Father through His Son.

130. It is hard to overestimate the seminal role of the drama inherent in the liturgy itself for the beginnings of liturgical drama in the West. Starting with small dialogues that were an integral part of the liturgical texts, such as that between Mary Magdalene and the angel at Christ's tomb, or that between Moses and God, liturgists soon found themselves adding dramatic tropes that began to be acted out, even with costume, and added to Mass or Vespers. Thus musical processions and Easter and Christmas dramas of striking beauty and immediacy were produced in religious communities and, eventually, in secular communities.

131. "Listen: There was once a king sitting on his throne. Around him stood great and wonderfully beautiful columns ornamented with ivory, bearing the banners of the king with great honour. Then it pleased the king to raise a small feather from the ground and he commanded it to fly. The feather flew, not because of anything in itself but because the air bore it along. Thus am I ..." (trans. Page, *Sequences*).

No one questions the honor they bestow, since by outside adornment may the spiritual be seen.

Even the colors are clear to me now, truly dazzling in their splendor. Faith wears brilliant scarlet, Chastity is in gold, holding a royal scepter with a white infant over her womb and a dove with outstretched wings brooding above her head. Unhappy Anima [Soul] begins in pure white, the sullied filth of the world rubbing against her with the oily filth of the Devil as the procession moves on—and there is the point: Even though the three Marys bore witness to a real change in the order of things, that newer and purer order is always being threatened and always needs defense in our mutable world. The victory of the sixteen female Virtues and their queen over the Devil is a manifestation of that always precarious struggle.

Nothing is repeated exactly in this music; nothing occurs the same way twice. My processional play exists not in eternal time, but in our time, which is the world of perpetual change, of mutability, of *musica mundana*. And how I love its continual surprises! Even the colors of their gowns will change from moment to moment as the light in the cloister church changes its angle and degree of penetration, as the candles burn down, as the dramatic action unfolds.

Last night I dreamed that I began teaching them the music. In the dream, they giggled and stumbled and behaved like sheep—no, more like goats. They hissed when the Devil appeared and rolled their eyes. Never mind. It is begun.

 Thinking more about the *Ordo* this morning, it seems ironic that Volmar, of all people, should be called upon to oppose all the Virtues, to vie with us and accuse us of wasting our lives. He, who was the first to understand that I needed to record the visions in writing before

132. Venerated since the 4th century as a

they paralyzed me—my amanuensis and *symmista*. In all of the bitter negotiating I did with Abbot Kuno, Volmar understood in his heart that he would come with me, that his own service to God had something to do with being of service to me. For him, it was simply a matter of waiting patiently until Kuno achieved the same clarity. And here I go casting Volmar in the role of Devil, the same Devil who opposes music and drags the wandering soul into the snares and temptations of worldliness!

But what alternatives do I really have? Aside from the real spiritual dangers of such a risk for most of the women, having one of them play the Devil is ludicrous in the extreme, for there simply is not in our voices that resonance and threatening power that I need from the Devil. Oh, we can be giddy and petty and shrill and frightening in all those ways that chill like icy winds along the spine, but not in the ways that rush plummeting into your bowels and make you examine your heart's true intentions. In fact, Volmar himself has told me that in several male monasteries where they have enriched their great Easter and Nativity feasts with graceful embellishments of the liturgy, the monks portray all of the characters, even the three Marys at the tomb.

But having monks take all of the parts is not so strange, after all, for there are men with such tender sensibilities as would make this possible—men, large and tall, bearded though they may be physically, whose voices surprise us with their sweetness and treble sound, and do so for the extent of their adult lives. Just so I heard many of the psalms and offices sung at St. Disibode's for more than forty years. The diversity among the men was sufficient to allow for antiphonal singing at the dia- pason[133] without sacrificing any melodic integrity.

martyr of the city of Rome, St. Laurence was a deacon under Pope Sixtus II during the persecution in Rome under Emperor Valerian. Tradition tells that he was executed by roasting, and so he is generally depicted with a gridiron and is honored as the patron saint of cooks.

▣ 133. Hildegard uses the term common to Greek and medieval music for the ratio 1:2, which we now identify as the interval

But the women, no. True, some of us have fairly expansive areas of sound. But others make only the most timid and timorous, birdlike scratchings, weak and without substance. There are those who seem to increase in volume in the higher reaches, seem to fill the surrounding air with sounds like wild dogs and piercing whistles. Others sound like warmly vibrating strings, and a very few have voices that sail into our valley with the quality of well-tempered bells pounded out of the most precious metals, that vie with Adam before the Fall in depicting the whole range of the heavenly spheres.[134] The variety and diversity is intriguing, and may even be linked to subtle differences in individual souls. It certainly supports and gives clarity to encouraging each of the female Virtues in my *Ordo* to differentiate herself not only by what she sings but also by the quality of sound she brings. Contemptus Mundi needs to be one of our older frog voices, proud and hoarse with a watery gargle, while Humilitas has not a simple, but a tempered sweetness; Discretio, a voice of controlled intelligence; and Castitas may surprise them all with the sensuous range and roundings of her passionate melodies.

Still, it is a far different thing from the kind of high-voice, low-voice division that characterizes the monastic choirs in men's houses. Also, men's voices have a natural carrying quality we cannot take for granted: With rare exceptions, men have only to open their mouths to sing, and a certain rich fluidity results. It has conviction and weight and a spiritual anonymity that is noble. It is easy on the ear of God, I think; but the ears of the prelates of Mainz will of an octave (acoustically, one tone has twice the vibrations per second as the other). Even when singing monody (as in chant), a choir composed of both men and boys regularly enjoys and exploits the contrast of sound afforded by the possibility of alternating their singing of a melody at the octave rather than in unison.

❧ 134. In several letters, as well as her medical treatise, Hildegard expressed her belief that what most characterized Adam before the Fall was the fact that he was capable of making and of hearing every possible musical sound, including those of the heavenly spheres.

be engaged by the variety and insistence of the sounds produced by each of the Virtues. The Devil will meet opponents who are passionate, penetrating, and tenacious, fierce in their abhorrence of evil, and merciless in their pursuit of God's justice through the heavenly harmony.

Later

 It is strange how different and muffled the Angelus sounds when the air is so still. It is already after Sext, but the fog remains, brooding heavily over the river, and even the extreme, fiery heat of the sun cannot burn it away as it usually does at least before None at this time of year. The air itself is oppressively viscous, with no movement at all. Whether from heat or from this pressure of the air, birds seem neither to fly nor cry nor call. It reminds me again of the initial stillness of my inner world.

That strangeness became more familiar through sound, but it didn't happen until I had been singing the liturgy with Jutta at St. Disibode's for many years. Already I had gathered courage sufficient to ask my dear teacher whether she also saw the moving pictures and appearances that presented themselves to my inner senses. Her gentle but negative answer, echoed also by my devoted *magister* Volmar, was bewildering to me, and it forced my inner world to retreat further into hiding. Now I deliberately hid the difference in me, away from the eyes of men in the outer world who might guess, intrude, and ridicule the strangeness in me. Then, for a while, its silence became shaming, and I began to seek it only in the times just before and after the offices and the singing of the Mass, when the sound of the chant would lend its own auditory beauty, clarity, and spiritual power to bring my silent world into liturgical time. This went on for some while, at least until my fifteenth year.

One evening, towards the end of First Vespers for the Vigil of the Annunciation, we had just finished the repetition of the antiphon for the Magnificat. In the quiet of the silent *Pater noster*, I heard a rich clear voice which said, "I am the Voice of Wisdom," and my beautiful inner world opened to the world of sound in the Shadow of the Living Light. Hers was a richly musical, but disembodied voice, for I could not yet locate Wisdom among the figures and tableaux that appeared to me. Yet the sound of her voice was a great comfort to me, and she began to explain many of the visions in great detail, sometimes telling the many levels of symbolic meaning not apparent to my inner eye.

It was much later that other sounds and voices gradually entered that world, making it always richer and—strangely—more familiar, while more filled with mystery. But then, periodically, the Voice of Wisdom would take on an admonitory tone, and I began to feel it in my body and dread her admonitions for the conflict it would cause in me. She might advise me to write down what I saw and heard, at first gently, then sometimes not so gently. There was often an insistence, a pressure in her commands that would actually feel like a dull, nasty blade pressed the length of my spine, threatening to crush into my pelvis and even into my legs. It would frighten and bewilder me; for years I didn't dare mention it to anyone, though several of my dear sisters and brothers in Christ observed the suffering of my poor frail frame and wondered at the punishment.[135]

The bell rings from the refectory, and I will read them Jerome's letter to Eustochium before Vespers.

135. Much of this material is related by Hildegard herself in the preface to her *Scivias*. For example: "I heard a voice from Heaven saying, 'I am the Living Light, Who illuminates the darkness.... O human, who receives these things meant to manifest what is hidden not in the disquiet of deception but in the purity of simplicity, write, therefore, the things you see and hear.' But I, though I saw and heard these things, refused to write for a long time through doubt and bad opinion and the diversity of human words, not with stubbornness but in the exercise of humility, until, laid low by the scourge of God, I fell upon a bed of sickness; then, compelled at last by many illnesses, and by the witness of a certain noble maiden of good conduct [Rikkarda] and of that man whom I had secretly sought and found, as mentioned above [Volmar], I set my hand to the writing." (Trans. Hart & Bishop, *Scivias*, p. 60.)

The light began to fail so quickly after First Vespers for Our Lady, I suddenly realized

August 15, 1152
Feast of the Assumption of
the Blessed Virgin

our long summer evenings are finished for the year. The dew has already fallen, and, if the lower fields had not been gathered as soon as they were cut this afternoon, the hay would have already started to mold where it lay. The moon clears the trees in the East as I watch, so heavy and full that it threatens to roll out of the sky with its own weight. Summer crops need harvesting and careful storage before the next, most orange moon of our year; the drying of herbs continues, and this year should see the beginnings of self-sufficiency for most of the necessities of our own dispensary.

It is the use of minerals and gemstones, most of all, that elude people's understanding. Their properties absorb heat and light from the sun, and then concentrate them even more than plants do. Their many-faceted surfaces reflect the source, just the way jewel-like flowers exude fragrance and therefore must have healing powers. We are so criticized for wearing, admiring, "attaching ourselves" to these incarnate jewels, without any sense of how deeply connected they are to the very Source and Fountain of Light. Surely there are mysteries mirrored here in the refractions of light itself, and who is to speak for the healings that have been accomplished with the use of these stones?[136]

I think of the glorious, cerulean blue sapphire, gold-flecked and laden with symbolic meaning for those of us who adore the stone most rejected, that *lapis* [stone] who is Christ, who becomes the cornerstone of the Heavenly Jerusalem. In the case of Sr. Radegund, green chalcedony is the stone I advise. It is not so much her periods of intractable pain that concern me, for such pain is familiar to most of us from time to time; rather, it is the loss of perception, of balance, the spells of dizziness, attacks of vertigo, the severity

136. Hildegard has classified the properties of twenty-five gemstones and details some of the medicinal uses and most effective physical placement in her *Physica* (*PL*, pp. 1247–66).

increasing to loss of consciousness on at least two occasions. And this in the one I have newly appointed prioress to replace Rikkarda, my lost lamb. In addition, I have trained her as cantrix, and made her responsible for preparing Christina and Gudrun for their Ceremony of Consecration on the Feast of St. Matthew, less than two months from now. Her symptoms are confusing. Perhaps they are due to her responsibility for teaching all of the younger ones the intricacies of psalm tones, my own criticism of some of the Office music in its lack of clarity, my impatience with their lack of understanding of images which have always spoken for themselves—a lack of hearing and "knowing" unconscionable for women of such noble origins and a betrayal of basic responsibilities of their vocation.

But her fainting on two occasions, just after the sequence and then while preparing to receive the Host at this Mass, is impenetrable. There is no one else to fix the altar Sacramentary for Volmar. Now that Rikkarda is gone, there is no one else who so deeply understands the significance and order of the ecclesiastical year, the dovetailing of fixed and movable feasts, or even the small triumph of knowing what is proper to any one saint versus what is required by the Season. How much better to allow Radegund—encourage her even—to wear the chalcedony over her breast, like a pectoral cross, to ring her delicate head with a crown of stones if necessary, in order to reinforce that passage of light and energy through a delicate, melancholic temperament. For if balance is overstepped so that, even in the act of contemplating the life of the Eucharistic gifts, her body and mind are overwhelmed, then conduits to prayer are indeed required.

Small cliff swallows dart deeply into the crevasses of the mountainside, their forked tails curiously airborne though Luciferan. Their perilous balance is achieved through an ability to encompass totality at any given moment. So let her green stone gather light from the sun, dense rays buried in the earth, and beams from distant stars and visible planets, if such concentration be required for her health and for the life of our music.

The pelican again appeared to me, her bleeding breast belying all that is whole and healthy in her plumage. She was brooding, as had Wisdom on the water, I mean shimmering over its surface with wondrous wings—I have seen them—like those of the seraphim, beating so rapidly, fanning the air in gold with a sound more like whispered litanies through fluttering eyelids, not lips, as if praying eyes themselves could fan the light to paint the golden wings of angels.

August 28, 1152
Feast of St. Augustine, Bishop and Confessor

But meanwhile, the grain is wet and molded from all the rain, stinking of that insidious fungus[137] that sneaks up on people's minds and thinking. This means that either I give way to the clamoring voices of my spoiled women who demand their potted meat, their spitted lamb and goat, or take the risk of ergot poisoning by insisting they go without meat entirely, which seems a foolish interpretation of the Rule at this point,[138] at least until the weather changes and the harvested grain is dry.

Perhaps it is worse for women's minds, since we are weaker to start with. Take for example what happened today during recreation, the time set aside from our usual silence, for sharing our humanity. I was walking in the cloister to exercise these limbs aching so from the persistent rain, seeking just a

137. *Claviceps purpurae*, or ergot, is a fungus found on grain, but particularly on rye, which was one of the most common grains used for bread during the Middle Ages. Large outbreaks of ergot poisoning were reported in Germany as early as the 9th century, involving hallucinatory experience and other symptoms of nervous disorder. As with any plant fungus, the proliferation of ergot was greatest during growing seasons having an excess of rain and dampness. Often called "St. Anthony's Fire," it was sufficiently prevalent in the 12th century to require the building of hospitals to treat those who suffered from the disease. (Kraft, *Eye Sees More*, p. 106, n. 102.)

138. *RB*, ch. 39: "Let everyone, except the sick who are very weak, abstain entirely from eating the meat of four-footed animals."

few minutes' intercourse with an escaped white cloud in blue sky before the gray deluge closed over again, when I overheard a shallow conversation between Christina and Radegund.

During recreation at Cîteaux, in Abbot Bernard's Cistercian house, I would no doubt be hearing heady philosophical arguments disputing the merits of Augustine's Ciceronian rhetoric or disquisitions on the theology of our Church Fathers, the real theologians. One of the monks in the community might be preparing to undertake a pilgrimage to Compostela, to follow that famous route through the Iberian mountains in order to see the true relics of St. James. Or the monks might be discussing more worldly things, but things affecting the state of the whole Church, like the cost of the Holy Jerusalem War. That is a matter for the Pope and the princes of the Church, although its military logistics may be accomplished by kings who need the spiritual arm of the Holy See behind them. Imagine the provisioning of an army, the moving of a royal household from West to East. Henry II of England or our German Frederick, taking a retinue from London overseas, or from Germany over land and then sea to the Holy Land. Feeding them all. Armoring them, or not, vesting some of them, feeding them bread, welding their arms, contracting the boats, all with the blessing of the Holy See.

At the Synod of Trier after the examination of my first writings, food seemed simply to appear, to be placed on the tables during the serious business of taking notes, listening, evaluating, waiting, being witnessed. Fascinating conversations among the delegates ranged through subtle theological symbolism in liturgy, musical practices, the finest points of the interpretation of the Rule. Everyone was fed. The Holy Father travels with a machinery, a retinue, and an organization so oiled and powerful it may extend back to the days when Rome was entertaining itself with the sacrifice in the circus maximus of Christian martyrs.

But, of course, this is sheer fancy. I, poor frail woman that I am, was not invited to Trier, so how would I know? Reports about my writing apparently went from Volmar to Abbot Kuno, from Kuno to Archbishop Henry of Mainz, from Henry to Pope Eugenius, with the added encouragement of his much-admired fellow Cistercian, Bernard, who was attending the Synod and knew of my work.

I never attended the Synod of Trier; rather, Eugenius III sent his legates to Disibodenberg to collect what writings I had so far completed. They were read aloud and examined in my absence, and I can only imagine the enormity of the preparations, the care and feeding of those important men, as I wrestle with the care and feeding of my own community now, five years later.

The greatest problem lies in trying to integrate everything, to invest all with meaning, see it all as part of a larger, more meaningful life. Let the food be simple and fresh, and let the lay sisters cook it and care for us, freeing my choir nuns for other things; but for what? Complaining about food? Arguing among themselves? The chattering conversation I overheard during recreation comes once again to mind. It seems to have been a reminiscence of two different houses, of two different childhoods, compared. On the one side was Christina, brimming with gifts and intelligence, recalling her repeated attempts to befriend a cranky scribe who was retained by her father to teach her brothers; also, her fascination with the shapes of letters, the sounds of phrases, not only of sung music but of spoken sounds, those that are carefully formed, rounded, reworked, and perfected out of love and vision. Her notion, opposed absolutely by her father, was that she might have been allowed to do more than pine while learning the arts of tapestry. She longed to extend the meanings and explorations of words themselves.

The other side came from Radegund, whose household, although equally as noble as Christina's, was relatively impecunious, its functioning precarious for lack of funds. Her father was off at the Holy War; her mother, unusually able, loved to make order in her diminished household. She created stewards' lists, planting charts, and maps of landholdings. The woman had not learned such things by gender or upbringing or any other training, but she accomplished them well. Such are the rare challenges and unlooked-for opportunities for taking responsibility, even developing the skills of reading and writing.

Still, compared with conversations that must take place at synods like Trier, or even at monasteries like Cîteaux, ours are more often petty, lacking the knowledge that provides at least aesthetic, if not theological, dimension. Instead of condemning women for their seemingly perennial weakness of thinking, imagine investing their lives and service with a seriousness of purpose, with goals equivalent to winning the Holy Land: birthing productive children, feeding their minds and hearts with learning. They could be challenged to produce and refine indigenous medicinals, tried for their efficacy, not used automatically because of Greek philosophical speculation about medicinal use of plants, slavishly copied into book after book without fresh trial.[139] Though physical ailments lack all nobility, are more an embarrassment in the eyes of the world than anything else, and a punishment in the eyes of the Church (witness Job), we would have our knowledge about disorders of the body, its causes and cures, recorded in our scriptorium. We would not go so far as to busy our scriptorium with adornment or illumination of works of a physiological nature. Gold and precious colors will be saved for divine mysteries and liturgical books; but the knowledge of our experience needs to be preserved. Our minds and hands will continue to be occupied with healing the body as well as the soul.

Today, nothing but mundane problems demand every bit of my attention, and I marvel at the philosophical speculations I've been able to consider and record here recently. The continuing, intense, and now untimely heat spoils even the food that is spiced as well as cooked. It sours our milk but thwarts the proper ripening of curd for making

September 8, 1152
Feast of the Nativity of the
Blessed Virgin Mary

139. Hildegard's isolated use of German words (as opposed to the Latin in which all of her works were written) for certain plants and medicinals in her two medicophysical

cheese. My women tire of overripe fruit. They complain about the heaviness of their black habits.

I am grateful for the thickness of our walls because they insulate us from the worst of the sun; but the herbs don't dry for all our careful gathering, sorting, and labeling, despite the strong sun, because the air is so filled with moisture, they mold. As do peaches, pears, and early apples. Certain of the grapes unacceptable for the last wine pressing, normally sun-dried to raisins, rot even on the vines, and I fear that our second-year harvest will disappoint us. So much for the recent efforts of the joiners and for the proud new ladders propped against the orchard trees, with all the rotting fruit dangling above them!

Creatures that fly and buzz and bite and sting collect around food, in the refectory, and even on ourselves. Daily odors of sweat that are usually at most sour have become so fetid that I have advised both Volmar and my sacristan to increase the use of incense. For now, we cense the choir for the Divine Office as well as for Mass. However, this evening one of my women fainted in choir at First Vespers for the Vigil of the Birth of Our Lady, and I must assume it was for lack of air to breathe and an excess of incense. The other possible reasons are more than I wish to consider at this juncture, although I continue always to ask for divine guidance in all such matters. Proper fasting is a blessed practice, but unnatural fasting, another thing; for when the human will grows so over-determined, the Spirit finds it hard to enter.[140]

treatises is strong evidence that her medical knowledge was empirical, rather than rote knowledge of what would then have been the standardized Greek sources, even supposing that Latin translations might have been available to her.

⬛ 140. Hildegard's views on excess fasting are strong and clear; for example, in a letter to the abbess of a Cistercian monastery at Wethderswinkele, she writes a polemic based on the metaphor of dry, arid, or overplowed land producing empty sham, as opposed to the kind of balanced nourishment necessary for *viriditas* and the development of the virtues, especially of humility and love (*PL*, pp. 319–20).

Once again I hear renewed complaints about the length of the vigils, the volume of music to be learned by the novices. Meanwhile, the amount of music to be learned for the Play of the Virtues continues to grow. The hymn for St. Ursula turns out to be long and complex, with new music for every stanza, and yet they do not fail in their enthusiasm for St. Ursula herself. Their devotion to the one true relic of hers that we house is as real as the bone itself. Inspired by her courage and vision, we all hunger for any and all information about her life; but one wonders about the revelations about her that continue to proliferate, coming now from Schönau, Deutz, Mainz, and Cologne itself. One begins to smell worldly gain more than divine source. The hysteria that mounts with the proliferation of saleable relics from the graveyard at Cologne does not sully our house, and I pray that the music I have received will honor her true nature when we sing it October 21st; for, although the women have protested difficulties learning the songs for Ursula in time for the offices of her feast day, I have no doubt it will be accomplished, even if I have to sing the sequence for the Mass myself.

It is, after all, simply an instance of *canticum novum* [new song], a kind of song renewed as it comes through me. We are exhorted always to come to Him with a new song, as we are told again and again each week in our singing of Psalm 150. What reason would we ever have to believe He loves only what is entirely familiar? Furthermore, when the words come, they are merely empty shells without the music. They live as they are sung, for the words are the body and the music the spirit.[141] Words and music become inextricable for me, and once I can hear the sound with absolute clarity through my inner ears, I can sing it with surety.

The real problem lies in teaching it, because the music I hear breaks through the customary qualities and divisions

141. "And the body signifies the word; truly the music manifests the spirit, just as the celestial harmony declares the Divinity and the word, the humanity of the Son of God." (*Scivias*, in *PL*, pp. 735–36.)

of the modes and generates a different kind of structure. No longer do the "ears of memory" suffice for my women; rather, their outer ears must familiarize themselves with, and then recognize, small shoots of melody which may then reappear shortly in another mode, at another pitch, slightly lengthened perhaps, elaborated or simply extended, always pushing the boundaries of our human, limited, female voices higher and higher until at some point, finally, only the very highest of them will be able to pierce the climaxing tones. But they are supported everywhere by these constantly changing, nourishing shoots, and, as the voices come down from the heights, they are joined once again by all the others for their earthly descent. Only in the sequences and hymns, the really extended pieces, is the range so demanding.

By comparison, the antiphons are simple and easy for the women to grasp. Today, Archbishop Henry sent two of his prelates from Mainz for a visitation on the Rupertsberg. They were here for the Divine Office when we sang one of my Marian antiphons, and it went well. Their interest is of course combined with what they feel is their duty to make certain that we continue to warrant their support, that our independence from St. Disibode's has not resulted in lapses in the Rule that women so often fall into. I trust they were satisfied by the end of Vespers.

 I did not expect that the arch- bishop himself would come this distance

September 21, 1152
Eighteenth Sunday after Pentecost and Feast of St. Matthew, Apostle and Evangelist

for the sake of celebrating the ritual Consecration of a Virgin for just two of my women. In fact, I am pleased that he has sent not only Bishop Karolus this morning, but his elaborate Pontifical as well, the book in which all the parts that are his to chant are included. The ancient ceremony has been repeated so many times—first at Disibodenberg and now at St. Rupert's—that most parts are lodged in my head and my heart; but, now that I am growing so fond of the fruits of scribal records, I enjoy seeing the physical plan on the page. I marvel at the care taken to flourish certain initials and paint them in many colors, to rubricate in red the beginning of each new sentence. Lines are inscribed with a stylus, straight and exactly parallel, then the curving strokes of uncial script break the perfect angularity of the lines at every juncture. It seems strange, but according to what Basel tells me, the Ceremony for the Consecration of a Virgin, so central to the life and purpose of Benedictine women's convents, has never been lodged in their own records or choir books.

In the bishop's Sacramentary, this ritual is surrounded by texts and *ordos* for the ordination of a bishop, dedication of a church, episcopal blessings of vestments, vessels, crosses, statues, bells, and weapons, expulsion of public penitents on Ash Wednesday and their reconciliation on Thursday of Holy Week, elevation of archbishop and cardinal, even the rites for excommunication and absolution. The choir music we sing, and the antiphons and responses of the consecrated one in dialogue with the presiding cleric, are borrowed from other feast days, primarily from the Feast of St. Agnes, and these we know well. Acknowledging the sanctity bestowed on the new vestments as blessed by the bishop, the virgins sing, as did St. Agnes, "God has clothed me with a robe woven with gold, and provided me with vast necklaces." Such is the glory that befits our poverty before God that my women always look so radiant in their veils, marked with the single cross embroidered in red.

Today both aisles are strewn with containers of flowers for the occasion, some filled with asters, pale lavender and white, looking like so many stars fallen from the sky of green fields where they grow, starting immediately to shed their hairlike petal rays as soon as they are picked. Never mind. They are only for today. Four varieties of goldenrod, boneset the color of good parchment, deep crimson roses, and the delicate, flowering stems from our bed of rampant mint may well cause the bees to swarm right into the church, through the open doors that bring green light from the outside. The smell of the mint is particularly pungent, adding its late September incense to the smoky odors that will precede my two virgins as they return from the sacristy clothed in their new vestments, singing together the wonderful responsory from St. Agnes's feast: ‡‡*I love Christ, into whose chambers I have entered, whose Mother is a Virgin, whose Father knew not a woman, and whose instruments sing to me with measured voices: whom when I shall have loved I am chaste, when I shall have touched I am clean, when I shall have received I am a Virgin. ℣. Honey and milk from His mouth have I taken, and His blood hath adorned my cheeks.*[142]‡‡

After Compline

 It doesn't always happen. Often we wait for it in vain. This time the colors of her body itself changed, the body being the garment of the soul. The two of them came, first with their garments to be blessed by Bishop Karolus, then with their newly clad selves, each time answering the bishop's call of "*Venite, venite, venite,*" inviting them to come forward into the fold, to be numbered among God's true aristocracy.

It was Christina who was transfigured by her consecration. Christina, whose parents so clearly despised her and who came so begrudgingly to the ceremony. She who was now in the habit of painting during her free time, a habit initiated and inspired by her stealing green pigment from the painter of our wall panels. Rebellious and even surly at times according to my own observation, but with gifts of pictures that pour from her fingers like ribbons of wax. Yet she cares little for what she does, only that she does it.

Thin and long boned, with a veil of dark hair we removed, Christina's being intimidates others easily, though her skills in some areas remain underdevel-

142. The verse of this responsory, originally inspired by the Song of Songs, was clearly in Hildegard's head when she composed the responsory for St. Ursula, whom she describes as "a dripping honeycomb/was the virgin Ursula/who longed to embrace the Lamb of God,/Honey and milk under her tongue...."

oped. Her participation in choir, for example, is erratic, and I would love to be able to depend on it more. The range of her voice is so much lower than her other sisters; it is nearly like having a male voice among us, and it is she to whom I assign the tenor that supports any organal singing we do,[143] she who will support the movement of the higher, piercing flying birds in my hymn for St. Ursula in October.

Her presence is commanding; she is abnormally tall. Her eyes, eaglelike, piercing but at the same time curtained, drawn inward to a more colorful landscape perhaps than the one I have pressed upon her service. We have rarely spoken about things of substance, except what I have formally taught. She is one of the few who came to us with Latin as well as common speech, and I encourage her now to concentrate her skills, to channel them into scribal duties, helping me with my ever-growing correspondence. She never fails to write with flourishes, adding here and there a border of flowers, acanthus leaves, or even watery shapes whose meaning is not clear, even to me. She has not been entirely happy in this work, nor I with her.

But it is to her own color we were all drawn at her consecration. The choral Propers of the Mass that had already been sung—the Introit and Gradual—were from the season of Lent, with their typically penitential character. Her solemnity and bearing as she approached with her long fingers wrapping the lit candles was striking, almost fierce. Briefly, the thought flashed through me that she might refuse, might renege, might push herself back into the world where she could so easily tower, and even reign with elegance as a countess or

143. Hildegard refers here to the musical form *organum*, in which monody (as in chant) first broke through into polyphony (more than one melodic line). In its most primitive form, one voice, usually the lower, holds a pitch while others sing an ornate melody in counterpoint. Often, during the 11th and 12th centuries, as in the case of Hildegard's compositions, the organal voice is implied, rather than written; the *tenor* ("held," from the Latin *tenere*) notes are drones whose pitches and occasional changes are determined by the movement of the ornate melody.

marchioness. The moment passed. Her usual deep voice seemed to originate somewhere in her knees, and then, as she suddenly dropped and prostrated herself, it became an even deeper buzzing sound.

Called into new being by the bishop, her face turned colors, but many colors, *circumamicta varietatibus* with the chosen queen of the psalm.[144] First her own hidden green, so strong now there was a general spontaneous movement among us to support her, the color of her face so green, and then mustard and rose and violet, to pure gold. She stood before us radiating from her body through her new garments, rained on by particled streams of gold penetrating the open doors and windows, tiny globules of gold dust dancing on the lids of her rapt eyes, her swan-necked hands and wrists articulating liquid shapes like two swarms of bees.

Finally, pressing in, we closed ranks around her, singing our office hymn of perfection, the *Veni creator spiritus* [Come, Creator Spirit] from Pentecost, knowing God's finger had touched this young woman, transformed her into a respected stranger among us, in the act of her binding herself to the community in perpetual service to God.

May God's gold infuse any books of ours she may decorate in glory.

September 30, 1152
Feast of St. Jerome, Presbyter[145]

 There can be no argument about cultivation of new vines, since nothing could be more productive on

144. From Vulgate Psalm 44:10, which describes the queen "clothed in gold, surrounded with variety," and again in verse 15, "All the glory of the queen is within, in gilded borders, surrounded in variety." Hildegard expands this image and then transfers it into the realm of sound in the climax of her hymn for St. Ursula, where Ursula's "innocent flock," her consecrated virgins, "shouted out in the most brilliant voice,/A sound of purest gold,/Of topaz, and of sapphire, all clothed about with gold." This is the same iconography found in the description of the woman in the Apocalypse who is "clothed in the sun" (*amicta sole*).

145. Outstanding scholar and a Doctor of the Church, Jerome (340–420) was

the steep hill-banks of our meandering river. All up and down the nearly vertical slopes, the soil is rich in minerals. It has supported little else besides the grazing of goats. That much is clear; and it would be foolish to encourage planting grain anywhere except on those lands deeded to us that lie much lower in the valley. We have revived an old orchard on the site of our cemetery whose apples and pears are only of fair quality, but whose quinces are outstanding in both their beauty and salutary uses. Mulberries, hazel, and chestnuts thrive on some of the lands we have at long last acquired from Disibodenberg; others, cleared and planted for years, support fruit trees of many varieties, including both cherry and plum. The soils vary widely from place to place, and the wine we have so far produced on our lands is light and fruity, its color remarkably clear. The same vines on the newly acquired lands, with soil that is clearly more acetic, may produce a wine that has even more fragrance, or

responsible for the text of the Latin Bible that Hildegard knew. He had command of Hebrew and Greek as well as Latin and began his revisions of Latin versions of Scriptures under the support of Pope Damasus, to whom he was secretary. Jerome was also an early supporter of the establishment of monasticism in the Western Church. He spent his last years in Bethlehem, where—with the help of Paula, a Roman widow and long-time student—he established a kind of double monastery which included a men's monastery headed by Jerome, a women's convent headed by Paula, a church common to both, a monastic school for boys, and an active scriptorium. In this setting and with the help of his well-trained scribes, Jerome completed his version of Holy Scripture that eventually received the title "Vulgate" or accepted text. Although there were no cardinals in the 4th century, Jerome is often depicted in cardinal's hat and robes, in order to indicate his ecclesiastical office in relation to Pope Damasus. Paintings and woodcuts usually portray him in the act of writing, with a large, thoroughly domesticated lion as companion to his scholarly activity. According to the *Acta sanctorum* (Acts of the Saints), the lion entered the monastery in Bethehem, terrifying Jerome's monks; thereupon, Jerome withdrew a thorn from the lion's paw, making the beast a friend for life.

whose taste remains more substantive when mixed with bitter herbs for medicinal purposes. Given our climate and stony riverbanks, I am increasingly convinced that more of our lands should be given to viniculture.

All of this came clear two weeks ago, when Volmar and I sat with all the deeds and maps spread out before us, piecing together our holdings like a gap-toothed puzzle. Many pieces are missing; yet, with each new dowry, there is the real possibility of filling in those gaps here and there, either by receiving lands as gifts or by using monies received to buy parcels we know to be contiguous and available. We might in time produce enough good wine on our lands for it to be a source of income, as I hear of at least one Cistercian house. Their success with vines is spoken of everywhere and may in time overshadow the production of the older Benedictine vineyards. To the west, at Trier, lie the lands held by the Benedictines of St. Matthias and St. Eucharius, to whose houses I have recently sent music in honor of their patron saints.[146] Their lands have produced good wines for centuries, perhaps even since the pagan Romans first took the area, for the habits of Roman soldiers are notorious: They were wild and extreme, and they drank wine and lusted to great excess.

According to St. Benedict's Rule, we learn the wisdom of moderation in all things, that the evil of wine lies in its abuse rather

146. Hildegard's hymn for Saint Matthias is *Mattias sanctus* (*Lieder*, #72, pp. 149–53). She wrote three songs for the Benedictine monastery of St. Eucharius: a responsory and a sequence for their patron saint (*Lieder*, #74 and #75, pp. 155–60) as well as an extremely powerful sequence for St. Maximin, a 4th-century bishop of Trier (*Lieder*, #76, pp. 160–63).

147. According to *RB*. Ch. 40, "a *hemina* [ca. ¼ litre] of wine for each monk each day is adequate we believe." In addition to the recommendations of Benedict, it is clear from Hildegard's writings that wine was an ingredient for many medications and tonics, and that both beer and wine were more safely consumed than water in many places. The main rule for fermented drinks was to "drink temperately."

than in its use, for what Christ consecrated for us as his blood in the Eucharist could hardly be evil. A half-pint a day St. Benedict recommends, outside of sanctified wine we partake from the chalice.[147] Its measure may vary further according to the season, the size of the person, the amount of labor produced, for wine is food as well as drink for our working bodies. Many of the medicinals we have learned to prepare and use constantly are more effective when the herbs are cooked in wine as a tincture; and wine is our best antiseptic for the cleansing of wounds. Even the green vines themselves have their uses. Those pruned out in the early spring are cut into pieces for tying up the main stems of grapevines as well as for training and securing other plants in need of support, for young grapevines are unusually pliable and yet strong by their nature. Their blossoming in June is an unfailing lure to swarming bees.

Across the river, on the east bank of the Rhine, the soil is congenial to the vines, much new wine is now produced to be sold, and last October and November we witnessed boats loaded with casks ready to be sold further to the south. So successful is wine production in this particular area that the Cistercians at Eberbach, as soon as a hectare of forest can be cleared, have it planted by their lay brothers, who serve as their own vinedressers and are naturally more productive than random peasantry. So impressive is their production of wine in this way, that they have received more and more benefices of land, some even at great distance from the monastery, where granges serve whole seasons as temporary housing for lay brothers; and I discovered recently that a bundle of new lands were given them by the archbishop of Mainz.

Our side of the river has not known a long tradition of growing grapes, and the fineness of taste required for profitable selling depends entirely on the various properties of the soil. The powdered stones we find in our own banks may not be as favorable as the chalky white marl that sustains such good taste in the mountains of southern Gaul. The same vines planted there, or in Trier, or even directly across the river, will produce grapes that taste very different when planted here, and so will the color and taste of our wine vary. These may be ambitious ideas, but with our numbers always growing, we have deep need to ripen to a fully secured autonomy.

Like the new Cistercian houses spreading out from Bernard's Cîteaux, we seem to be petitioned more and more by young adults, and the character of our novitiate continues a change already underway during the last years at St. Disibode's. Whereas I was given as a child into Jutta's care, so that I was formed entirely by the ideals of an anchoress and by the Rule of the Benedictines of the community that housed us both, how different it is now! Here at St. Rupertsberg, the head of a family may arrive at our gates offering a young woman in her twenties, and I as abbess find it challenging, difficult, and sometimes nearly impossible to pull such a fully grown woman through the rigors of our novitiate.

It is true, several of these women have proved extraordinarily capable; some worldly responsibilities are successfully transferable. Anna is proving a skillful cellaress; since I named her just two months ago, nutrition has improved, crops somehow reach us on time from farmers on our tenancies, and there is order for the first time in both kitchen and storage areas. The managing she did on her father's lands at a young age when her mother died, her father unconcerned with the running of the household, is all to our benefit.

For others, having been formed in the world means having acquired worldly values deeply ingrained, perhaps intractable in one or two. If they are then consecrated before these values are rooted out, the ancient ritual of their clothing becomes a sham, simply a way of covering them over, instead of initiating a perpetual inner conversion to God. Lacking that crucial devotion to *contemptus mundi*, worldly thoughts and desires sharpen to become a continuous form of temptation. My new prioress, Rikkarda's successor, reports finding clothing and jewels secreted in two straw-filled pallets in the area for novices. And, of course, they are the same two novices who complain that our pallets are not soft enough to afford them decent sleep, the same women who complain about rising at 3 A.M. to sing the

Nocturns and responsories now that Matins is in its proper hour for the season. I wonder what will happen when the freezing nights return and how we will get them into their choir stalls then?

Clearly, anticipating problems is a temptation of mine, which I will root out with thanksgiving, for I had today a chance to view with my own eyes these landholdings of ours. Riding out with Volmar as soon as the day's Mass was dismissed, my eyes followed with joy the curved, scalloped ribbons of goldenrod still blooming next to the lavender of asters and of joe-pye weed, fluffy and pale as it matures into its gone-to-seed stage. Patches of yellow leaves lit many trees, and bold vermilion creepers wound around trunks and threaded through evergreen boughs of our blue-green cedars. The air now is remarkably like clear water; the light, a pale rose. Apple and quince trees support ladders for picking, and grapes are pendulous, of a matte gray-green like weathered copper, ready to be collected in canvas and leather buckets, oaken barrels. The fecundity of this glorious spot of ours, sacred to St. Rupert whose precious bones are buried since the time of Boniface, is just another confirmation of the correctness of our move here, a justification of all the pain and illness it caused me to convince Abbot Kuno that it was not willfulness or worldly desire on my part to establish an autonomous community of women, that my visions were the gift of God and fully supported this venture; nay, inspired it from the first.

This afternoon I thought the precise diagonal rows of newly planted wine grapes spoke eloquently of our own growing culture on this mountain, in contrast to those curved ribbons of wildflowers. Planted, pruned, and fertilized to fecund maturity, they speak of planning, training, and priorities in our lives as opposed to the chaotic sensuality of nature, which I also love.

 The colors on our mountainside remind me how little time remains for gathering this year's medicinal plants. Already the tender perennials

October 18, 1152

Feast of St. Luke, Evangelist

have blackened in the first frosts, dying annuals blaze, and even the hardier mints and artemisias are ragged and no longer fit for our insides. Vines that cling to the trees are still brilliant scarlet, some beech trees are still green, while mulberries are almost transparently butter-yellow. It is the quality of the light in October that creates this palette—the sun's angle and placement in the sky as it illuminates the last leaves.

St. Luke as physician was the theme of my teaching to the women in chapter today, the subject of my own meditation as well. I tried to impress upon them that wisdom in the soul is necessary for healing the body. I wonder if we will ever have the kinds of facilities for healing the sick that we had at Disibodenberg, where the hospice was one of the largest buildings, heated by three ample fireplaces; not many came to our remote hilltop to stay as guests en route to somewhere else, but the sick and ailing found us and took refuge in what healing we could provide, some with torn flesh and some torn in ways less visible, but still responsive to the herbs and tinctures we used, the poultices we made. Jutta encouraged me, and the sights and smells grew less offensive the more skill I developed in treating them.[148]

If my women could understand the physician as friend to death, perhaps they could understand St. Luke's vision of the *Nunc dimittis* [149]—the long

148. In a paper delivered at a conference on Hildegard sponsored by the National Cathedral in Washington, DC, in January 1989, John Riddle, historian of medieval medicine and pharmacology, spoke of Hildegard's time as "apprentice in the dispensary" at Disibodenberg and also gave extensive linguistic evidence for her empirical knowledge and practice of medicine and pharmacology.

149. Known as the Song of Simeon (Luke 2:29–32) whose text is, "Now thou dost dismiss thy servant, O Lord, according to thy word in peace: because my eyes have seen thy salvation, which thou hast prepared before the face of all peoples, a light to the revelation of the Gentiles, and the glory of thy people Israel." The other two New Testament canticles are also taken from Luke's gospel: the *Benedictus* or Song of Zachary (1:68–79), which is sung at Lauds, and the *Magnificat* or Song of Mary (1:46–55), for Vespers.

loneliness of old Simeon's waiting and, finally, his joy at being able to welcome death peaceably, having seen his hope manifest in the person of the infant Jesus. They are mostly too young. God knows there is no one to inherit my crozier now that Rikkarda is gone, and I shudder to think of what could happen at my death; I need to give more thought to these things. Practical matters are at me all the time, and the feast that pulls most for my attention approaches fast. We will try to have all my new songs for St. Ursula on the 21st; those for the Divine Office are already well in hand, though the women balk at the words of my hymn *Cum vox sanguinis* [When the voice of the blood]. They don't understand them. They don't understand them because they haven't experienced divine mysteries on that level. We will sing the hymn regardless, and we will sing it at both First and Second Vespers. At the night office, the great events of her life will be narrated. I myself will chant the tripartite *passio* during the second Nocturn; the old *sermo*, during the third.[150] Not only will these serve as inspiration for the few among my own who have embarked upon their own voyages; they may also quell the current, generalized ground swell of grumbling and help them all to understand what *contemptus mundi* could require of any of us.

I fear that what I have so far heard of Elisabeth's visions at Schönau elaborate details too fantastic for the minds of most, fanning the traffic in relics more than feeding us from the inside or informing us with a special way of knowledge. My visions tell me of mysteries greater than all the combined details of the slaughter of Ursula and her 11,000 companions: passion that is devotion, consummation,

150. In monastic life, the long night office of Matins was the place where writings appropriate to the life of a particular saint's feast would be most in evidence. The life (*vita*, or *passio* if a martyr) would be divided among three of the Lections (or Readings) of the second Nocturn (followed by responsories), and a sermon (*sermo*) by or pertaining to the life of the saint would be divided among the Lections of the third Nocturn. For an English version of the text of the ancient *passio* that Hildegard might have read or chanted to her nuns, see Sheingorn & Thiebaux, *Passion of St. Ursula*, Toronto, 1990.

and steadfast love. Elisabeth has recently written that she is slandered and misunderstood and looks to me for sisterly support. I can sympathize; nevertheless she is imprudent, without *discretio*, and I fear she will unwittingly serve those whose coffers overflow from the sale of those beautiful heads and lustrous bones so revered in Cologne. The elaboration of such details says little to illuminate Ursula's courage when the forces of worldly men are thrown up against her in jeers and actions.

My texts in her honor are everywhere concerned with these matters. And if my women balk at the demands of my new music, it is probably because of its physical and emotional range. Let their boundaries be stretched! Why should we not be the vessels joining heaven and earth, soaring with the highest eagles and dipping down again like old buzzards at the dropped carrion or seed? There are at least five of us in the *schola* who can produce such sounds and stretch such a line. Let the *schola* carry my hymn for St. Ursula—an inspired gift of the Most High throughout—and the rest will be responsible only for the short antiphons that frame the psalms for all the offices of her feast. Each narrates a small portion of her outward journey, their music is simple, and they are easy to learn. It is not necessary that every one of them understand, but Mother of God bless me with two or three women who can appreciate what has spoken powerfully through me, so that we can be inspired in our own vows by the mystery and majesty of an Ursula. The cold, lonely going-out required to realize any vision binds me to this woman's story, and her struggle continues the terrible demands that were made on Abraham, on Moses, on all of us forced to go into the loneliest places—like the pelican—in search of the face of God, weighted with our own living bodies and daring to come out with more than ourselves.

 It was glorious, exhausting, and entirely fitting!

October 21, 1152
Feast of St. Ursula & the 11,000 Virgins

Never have we had so many people from the town of Bingen for Mass in our church; and today some came even from Cologne to hear our songs for St. Ursula, her story chanted, her life and passion joined, through Christ, in our own humble bodies.

The journey of Ursula is alive on our walls, and the panels glowed fiercely in the light of the scores of candles ensconced beneath them. The same narrative antiphons we use for the Divine Office function beautifully here as well. We processed from panel to panel as we sang antiphons and the psalms they framed; we recounted her journey as a grand procession preceding the Mass itself. Then, after Volmar had chanted the epistle, the Alleluia was sung, and finally came the moment for my gift to her, to Ursula as our most passionate Mother Church, the Beloved in the Song of Songs, the *sponsa christi* [bride of Christ], and our consummate exemplar of the woman whose powerful vision, though mocked in the eyes of the world, was strong enough to carry thousands of women on a pilgrimage requiring extraordinary courage. At the last moment, it was I alone who sang the sequence *"O Ecclesia,"* and not the *schola*, even after the many days of feverish preparation.

Never mind; it has been sung and heard, and it hallows the inner space, the stone walls of our newly functional church. Her substance, her bits of bone in our reliquary may not be imbedded in our altar, for St. Rupert's bones occupy that place of honor, but her reliquary is exquisite: her vision is deeply engraved in the metal, and seven lustrous gems further adorn both front and back.

The hymn, sung as a choral piece, was ragged, and it was fortuitous that I designated some of the women to sing an organal, drone voice at several of the most difficult points. We have one more chance to sing the hymn as a group this evening at Second Vespers. Even I know what a struggle this is, how few of my women can float their voices in the empyrean where the most glorious text lies, where the sound is one of most precious jewels surrounded in gold, like the woman clothed in the sun. It seems the only way I can get the richness here is by having some of them sing a drone, reinforcing the melody at those intervals sacred to Pythagoras and Boethius, that harmonize the heavenly choirs of angels, even the spheres themselves. The cheironomy for the piece is perhaps distracting them from the wonderful mysteries embodied here; the text should be an inner dance of contemplation, and I would hope that when next year we sing it, the *schola* can manage without my hand and arm being quite so obtrusive.

The river is always behind my eyes when I listen to the piece with my inner ears. The piece is filled with water, with the water journey, with the blood and water of sacrifice. Rarely do I actually take the time to observe the Nahe, or the Rhine; nevertheless, it is that sea journey to death that moves the line, far beyond the control of my good right arm, and it is that sense that always fails my women when left to their own devices. Sometimes they are so bloodless, and I wonder where I am taking them, and whether I am truly going alone, and I continually ask the most Blessed Virgin for reassurances about my flock, though I know there can be none.

Next comes my own devastating crash of spirits which I plan to avert by working hard on the Order of the Virtues. Having placed it on our calendar as part of this Advent-Parousia cycle, its date assigned as December 27, Feast of St. John the Evangelist, I pray it be infused with the sacred spirit of the Fourth Gospel. Our presentation of the *Ordo* will take the archbishop completely by surprise, and I pray that it may also be the authentic Word of God. As one by one the female Virtues identify themselves, and array themselves against the powerful forces of evil embodied in the Devil, the archbishop and those prelates who accompany him will begin to grasp the deep spiritual level from which this comes.

 The reasons are too ob-
scure to justify more
formal investigation. It was
Volmar who brought it to my attention, and with his usual diplomacy. No need to name names: Suddenly I knew her as an

October 28, 1152
Feast of SS. Simon and Jude

instigator. Volmar insists that the problem is fed by jealousy, and he, after all, is our confessor; but what comes brutally to my attention, finally, now that I am faced with it, is her searing anger. Not that she has expressed anything to me directly. In many ways that would be easier, because it might clarify the problem. Instead, a cauldron of some stinking brew simmers under the surface between us, while superficially she maintains to perfection her promise of obedience.

I suppose I might have been more attentive to the source of the complaints that my women have had over the last two years, but it has been absolutely necessary for me to retain what is positive and to move forward. I never expected they would remain cheerful in the face of such a difficult beginning. In all of our struggles to civilize the wild mountain terrain we have finally acquired, the physical discomforts we have withstood, and the dogged persistence with which we have had to sing our rounds of psalms and offices, day and night in makeshift quarters as the skeleton of our cloister church took shape, I was not surprised by their regular complaints. Given the high-born houses of origin my women have left behind, and the easy assurance of the basic requirements of regular food and shelter for those who had been part of our little community at Disibodenberg before we came here, small wonder that many have been discouraged these two years.

I knew that their discontents were born of fatigue, physical discomfort, and lack of the secure regularity that sustains the monastic life; and I saw their murmurings as small brushfires, snaking through the undergrowth and occasionally flaring up with great energy as we encountered particular crises. Therefore, the way I have dealt with the fires that have erupted periodically during our new life at St. Rupertsberg has been to contain them and let them die out, at the same time treating the real causes with all of the energy, intelligence, and prayer I could gather, knowing that our stability depended on my women seeing regular, rapid progress as a recognized functioning community.

What had not occurred to me was that one of my own women might be regularly fanning the fires and that—if Volmar is correct—she does it as a kind of spoiler, out of jealousy; and is it then jealousy of my freely elected, God-given, and extremely lonely authority over the rest? Indeed, my vision for this autonomous women's convent must be greater than any of theirs, as is my recognition of their individual gifts and their best possible expression in the community. Nevertheless, all of our intentions must be in agreement. Together we must abide in faith, praise God, continually praise and petition Him and His Mother to help us to flourish according to the Rule of St. Benedict. Our observance of the Rule must be regular and consistent. My faith must be that it is the hand of God that guides me here and fills me with visions for the instruction of the faithful, that the tongues of fire of the Holy Spirit inform my decisions for our future as St. Benedict's Rule shapes our days.

But my sister in faith would suggest to them otherwise about my leadership. In my presence, her anger is like ice, though she is supple and animated with the others, as I've observed her in conversation during recreation time. Her hands darted like swallows when she threaded the complicated lampas weave[151] on the loom, sketching the pattern on wax tablet in advance of its execution for my approval. For the weaving itself she has chosen the most dexterous and quick to assist in the work, assigning their places in the project and artfully teaching the craft to each of them in turn. In all of these tasks I have encouraged her, and I have allowed her far greater exercise of control over others than I might, genuinely admiring her

151. One of the more complex and decorative possibilities to be found in medieval textiles, lampas is a particular weave in which "the background is formed by the main warps and wefts, while the pattern is formed by weft floats secured by a binding warp. In other words, one set of warps and wefts forms the background while another set forms the pattern. The variation in weave between these areas causes them to reflect light differently and have different textures." (Martin, *Textiles*, p. 62.)

skill and rewarding her initiative, all in appreciation for the work accomplished for the good of the community.

She was already a young woman when she joined us in our last years at Disibodenberg, and she brought her skills with her. She had learned to weave as a child, at her mother's knee, in her father's baronial house, but she had had no opportunity to exercise this art with us until we began the simple Lenten cloth last winter, on a loom presented as a gift by her family. I myself told her the details I had heard about the alb worn by Barbarossa at his recent crowning, so she was already inspired by that when she had the opportunity to study firsthand the gowns worn by Archbishop Henry and the prelates from Mainz who served with him at the dedication of our church. Anyone visited by the royal household notices that it is not the impressive strip of gold brocade stretched along the broad hem of King Frederick's perfect alb—which of course priests wouldn't wear—that so amazes; rather, it is the fineness of the weave itself, of white linen so smooth and lustrous it could be silk; and so it was with the albs we saw in procession here in May.

Even now I recall the physical flush of excitement I felt when she suggested shortly afterwards that we ourselves weave some fine fabric for clothing the Virtues in the *Ordo* performance. We compared what we had each observed about the construction of the fine albs of the prelates. (They were made of very broad lengths of cloth, so they required few seams.) Sometime later, when the weaving was already underway, I discussed the matter with Basel during one of his periodic stays at the dispensary. It was he who told me about the beautifully shaped gussets under the arms and the panels of tiny pleats at each side, on the level of the knee, which give perfect freedom of movement for both legs and arms in procession and ritual.[152]

152. An alb similar to the one described can be seen at the Rijksmuseum Het Catharijneconvent in Utrecht, The Netherlands. It is in near-perfect condition and the only medieval imperial alb conserved in its entirety; it was probably given by Frederick Barbarossa to the Church of St. John in Utrecht on one of his three visits to the city.

He encouraged me to allow her to pursue the project, since it was in such perfect accord with the visions I had had about the clothing of the Virtues.

It was she who enabled us to secure the great quantity of linen thread, which was again a gift from the estate of her family. It was her idea that the thread remain in its natural, undyed state for the weaving. Only after each garment was sewn would it be dyed, the color for each Virtue a different hue, as I had envisioned it. Creating the iridescent effect of the lampas weave was her own inspiration, threading the loom with one set of warps and wefts for the background while another set formed the pattern. The variation between them produces two different textures, each of which reflects the light differently.

Her energy for the task seemed inexhaustible, and I never questioned her activity and dedication. It is only now that I begin to catch the whispered goad behind the complaints of those less quick of hand and mind whom she has instructed for the task: ‡‡ *The Lady Abbess wishes to advance herself in the eyes of the prelates. Our* domina *wishes to glorify herself in the colors of our toil. Our mother in Christ drives us unmercifully for her own sake, for the sake of her own name....*‡‡ Is it possible that the whispering is my own sheer exhaustion, allowing the Devil to tempt me again into doubting my own vision? The trials here are endless, and some, like the heartbreak of Rikkarda, and like this, are unanswerable, for the jealousy Volmar observes in her is not of my outer accomplishments, station, or authority, but of my inner spiritual state.

The trial will continue until she yields her quarrel with grace, nor will I succumb to temptation, and the Virtues will be clothed in mantles of great variety, in cloth of fine weave.

 The news of Rikkarda's sudden death arrived during the midday meal. It was my turn to read in the refectory, and I had barely begun; but I knew as soon as

𝔉riday, 𝕺ctober 31, 1152
𝔈ve of 𝒜ll 𝒮aints

I heard the sharp sound of the hooves of the messenger's horse on the frozen, rutted road up the mountain that leads to our gate. I may even have known before Lauds, getting up long before the cold dawn with stabbing in every joint, a strong harness of pain around my rib cage, and a stone in my heart. Every circular segment of my throat ached, and the impulse to moan from each far outweighed the desire to sing Lauds, praise Him, or even support my poor bones. Brother Nicholas had ridden all day without food in freezing rain in order to deliver the letter from Archbishop Hartwig of Bremen—her brother and my enemy. As the exhausted Nicholas whispered hoarsely to me, I heard several of my women gasp aloud and realized that my frame had simply gone down under the weight of the news. It was as if I were sinking through the earth. I remember seeing my hands, suddenly agitated and fluttering like so many sparrows, strangers to my arms and trunk. Low-angled winter light played shadowed patterns against the wall. Parts of me disengaged, had no center, and flew about; at the same time something vital had frozen. I felt that if I did not try to make a definite movement, and speak as well, my body and all my senses would disintegrate like a heap of clay shards. With enormous effort, I found a piece of my voice way under my belly and dragged it up with the suggestion to Brother Nicholas that we walk outside. From my women whispers, buzzings, and a few choked-off sobs pushed against my ears as we left the room. In the letter, her brother personally attested to the fact of her death and informed me that she had made her confession, been anointed with the holy oil and, "committing herself to the Lord through His Mother and St. John three times in the sign of the cross, confessing the Trinity and the Unity, died in perfect faith, hope and charity, I am sure, on the 29th of October."[153] I asked only the few questions that befit an abbess, not able to ask the ones that still press me—about the small details of how she died, the looks and smells of her adopted monastery, how she looked as Lady Abbess and what it sounded like when she, with her large frame and beautiful   153. *PL*, pp. 161–62.

movements, tapped her abbatial staff to begin an office. Did her women's voices respond in sweet, sure arcs of sound? Did their eyes seek the approval of her steady gray eyes, simultaneously deep and piercing? They were always like that.

They were always like that even at Disibodenberg, when she first arrived. Our blessed teacher Jutta was still very much alive at the time. I remember walking with Rikkarda during afternoon work period. We were sent to find belladonna and the mushrooms that eased the pains of the two men dying in our dispensary. The infirmarian trusted me to avoid the destroying angel (*amanita virosa*) that so much resembles the medicinal variety, because I identified mushrooms on the basis of their spore patterns as well as particulars of size, shape, and smell. We walked for a hundred paces in deep silence, searching the ground at our feet, then saw the valley that lay beyond the orchard and the woods that circled our monastery, which form a dome on the top of the hillside. It was a shock to walk out of those thick rock walls that contained us in safety and see the almost immediate steep drop down the sides of our sanctuary. The ribbon of a road that spiraled through the dense woods to the meadow below seemed like the only boundary between us and the rest of the world, between the solidity of the buildings that formed the organized pattern of our community at the top and the random scattering of a few farm buildings that poked up here and there out of a clearing of meadows thousands of meters below us. The dizziness of the shock recurs, and it is deadly. It is death, Mother of God, and there is no medicine.

 The news of her death must have been like a puncture wound in my chest through   Saturday, November 1, 1152   Feast of All Saints

which breath escapes, for I feel I am still collapsing in upon myself. I can neither sing nor speak aloud. Radegund was cantrix for today's

Office and Mass, as she was last evening at First Vespers. I will not cantor Sunday's liturgy either, but will shepherd my strength for night Matins, when we shall honor her directly by singing the Office for the Dead. I had not thought I would live to place her among the souls of the departed. ‡‡ Matins, I Nocturn, Lesson ii (Job 14:1–6): *Man born of a woman, living for a short time, is filled with many miseries. Who cometh forth like a flower, and is destroyed, and fleeth as a shadow, and never continueth in the same state. And dost thou think it meet to open thy eyes upon such an one, and to bring him into judgment with thee? Who can make him clean that is conceived of unclean seed? Is it not thou who only art? The days of man are short, and the number of his months is with thee: thou hast appointed his bounds, which cannot be passed. Depart a little from him, that he may rest, until his wished-for day come, as that of the hireling.*‡‡ I was unprepared. She was so young and terribly strong. The brutality comes not from death, but from its unexpectedness. It is as if all the righteous and justifiable anger I had been carrying around for so long were the lining of a large pig bladder that had stretched tighter and ever tighter with the passage of time. Now it has burst, and I move in a vacuum. ‡‡*Deliver me, O Lord, from eternal death, in that dreadful day, When the heavens and earth are to be moved, When thou shalt come to judge the world by fire....*[154]

Absolve, we beseech thee, O Lord, the soul of thy servant Rikkarda, that, being dead to this world, she may live to thee: and whatever sins she has committed through human frailty, do thou wipe away by the pardon of thy merciful goodness. Through our Lord Jesus Christ.[155]

℣. *Eternal rest give to her, O Lord.*
℟. *And let perpetual light shine upon her.*
℣. *May she rest in peace.*
℟. *Amen.*‡‡

154. Responsory for III Nocturn, Lesson i. The psalm-like words are as if spoken by the deceased.

155. Prayer from Office of the Dead, followed by concluding versicles (℣.) and responses (℟.)

Suddenly the symptoms descended. Or so I suppose, because I am al-

ready their too-familiar victim, ignorant of exactly when and how they began, and frozen into the paralyzing pains all over again. Any stronger pain in my knees will force me to lie flat. The bad taste in my mouth—chalky and dry and foul all the way from my gut—doesn't go away with herbal rinses. A filmy residue collects in each irritated eye and then dries like a hard crust of bread. The eyes itch fiercely. The joints of my fingers are shiny, swollen, and unbearably tender; even holding the stylus as gingerly as possible is extremely painful, and the movements and impressions I record on the wax tablet are nearly indecipherable. Turning my head becomes unbearable, my lower back pulls more and more, sitting is terrible, and going from sitting to standing is worse. The closer to the ground I remain the better; were it not for my knees, a position of continual prayer would be safest.

Quick winter sunset. Now it is pitch-dark and the decision must be made for someone else to cantor Vespers and Compline today; they must bring me straw wrapped in pillowcloths, heated coals and irons. I will attack this wracking body with warmth, prop it into a manageable position, and sing myself alone into the evening of the world.

The bells tell me the offices have been sung. My candles, though they sputter in the cold wind that leaks into the room, are still lighted, the shadows a dancing comfort bobbing and turning on the hangings that line my walls. I begin to sense the possibility of sinking into my own inner source, to see the flicker of the Shadow of the Living Light. Not that it ever goes away entirely, but I do have to allow it to come fully into my awareness, clear away the debris that hides it from me, whether worldly responsibilities, nagging personal complaints, harsh criticism, or even the confusion of the chaotic sounds that have surrounded us for over a year here as basic shelters are fixed and fitted out.

Intense pain can also obscure it, though I have often gotten through the pain to the light. When that happens, it is as though I have first to go through my physical body, pain by wracking pain, forgetting neither the nausea nor the tight catches in my breathing. Thus catalogued and acknowledged, located, joined and mapped like a pilgrimage, the physical symptoms convert themselves to sounds, jaggedly separate and screeching at first, each crying out for its hearing to predominate as they are scanned. Then, if I push on with this prayerful search, the roaring taxonomy of pains begins to coalesce, to symphonize itself, coming into a droning, but strangely fluid harmony of such an arrangement that the Shadow of the Living Light melts the various shapes into swirling building blocks, sculpting out of sound and light a brilliant architecture.

And then the crystalline voice emerges out of the landscape of articulated, moving parts. It is the Voice of Wisdom, she who has been with God from the beginning, from before the Fall, from beneath the Day Star. And her voice tells me that the time of mourning is past, the time of righteous anger no longer necessary, for God Himself has declared His passion for His best beloved and taken her against the snares and temptations of the world that were trying to claim her, those that promoted worldly ambition and simony, those that tempted her into disobedience.

The Voice of Wisdom swells to bell-like resonance. It fills my head and beyond, to reverberate from the candlelit walls that enwomb me here. It is remarkable to see in this light how Rikkarda is loved by the Beloved. All those who loved her in her bodily nobility, and I in my gratitude, my dependence on her human competence and diligent support, in my battle with the lords of the world clothed as prelates and clerics who took her from me, we are all as nothing compared with the powerful embrace of the King who had chosen her from the very beginning, whose love is so fierce in its heat that infused circles of boiling light rotate around her within a giant aureole. As beautiful in death as in life, she rises ravished and ravishing in the encircling light until she merges with the path of the sun. Poor golden sun, whose jealous splendor couldn't leave her behind for a fading moment of night or even a single shadow of dusky sunset, but must carry her with him to the ends of the earth and beyond to the East and the gates of Paradise itself! There he plants her, deep tree in the garden, roots nuzzled into the earth, the glinting waters hungry to nourish while branches above flourish fruit, leaves, and cascading flowers in bowers of perpetual bridal splendor.

 Meditating again upon her brother Hartwig's letter brings consolation now.

November 23, 1152
Last Sunday after Pentecost and Feast of St. Clement, Pope and Martyr[156]

Strange that I see and understand things in it today that are so different from the pain and shock of the news brought hastily from that ambitious prelate in Bremen nearly a month ago. Then, I was struck helpless by the fierce untimeliness of her death, and I suffered deeply from the knowledge that rankling differences had been left hanging between Rikkarda and me (not to speak of the anger I harbored against Hartwig).

I could barely hear or read, and then only with relief that she did not die unshriven; that she had been confessed and anointed in perfect faith. Now I understand even that she loved us, loved us and intended to see us again. His letter says: ‡‡ *So I ask you with all my power, if I am worthy to ask, that you love her as much as she loved you. And if she seems to have failed in any way—since this was due to*

156. Clement of Rome, so identified to differentiate him from his contemporary, the theologian Clement of Alexandria, was venerated as a martyr in the medieval Church. As bishop of Rome (pope), Clement wrote a letter to the church at Corinth ca. 96 to settle a fierce quarrel that had erupted over the deposing of certain presbyters in the congregation. The letter provides rare information about the history of the church at Corinth and is the first-known instance of papal intervention in the conduct of regional churches. A legend recounts the story that he was martyred by being tied to an anchor and thrown into the Black Sea, which accounts for the presence of an anchor in his iconography.

me, not to her—that at least you consider the tears she shed for having left your convent, tears that many people witnessed. And if death had not prevented her, she would have come to you—the permission had only just been given.[157] ‡‡ Lord knows what I am to make of it all, how much Hartwig can ever again be trusted when his worldliness is common knowledge; even now he tries to control those things that he is not fit to touch.

Still, something is required of us. The Introit we sang for the Mass today speaks clearly of bringing scattered exiles home;[158] the Gospel chants with terrible surety the coming of the Last Days, the chaos at the end of time, before the Parousia.[159] It is urgent that we do what is fitting for her. In five days, on November 28, just between this last Sunday of Pentecost and the First Sunday of Advent, it will be the prescribed thirty days from the day of her death, and I will ask my dear Volmar to do a Requiem with me, for Rikkarda.

Had we her precious body and blood at St. Rupertsberg, if, at the end of the Absolution, we could bear her dear body aloft among us, process her down to our own cemetery as we did with Matilda, our last canticle would be accompanied by the few winter birds—hawks, crows, and a single owl—that remain! Matilda we bore proudly among us to the happy caroling of our bells, all the way to the verdant June richness of the cemetery with its orchard veiled in pink. We sang *"Credo quod redemptor meus vivit"* [160]

157. Translation by Dronke, *WWMA*, p.

158. On the basis of the last sentence quoted above, people have suggested that Rikkarda intended to rejoin Hildegard's convent, but it is much more likely that her brother's letter reported an intended visit.

158. "Peace, the Lord says, not suffering, is the lot I send you; I will listen when you cry out to me, and bring scattered exiles home." (Jeremiah 29:11–14.)

159. Matthew 24:15–35.

160. "I believe that my Redeemer liveth, and in the last day I shall rise out of the earth, and in my flesh I shall see God my Savior. ℣. Whom I myself shall see, and not another, and my eyes shall behold." (Processional, taken from Office of the Dead, I Nocturn, Responsory i.)

and contributed handfuls of sunwarmed soil to her resting place. Rikkarda's Requiem will be different: wintercold, stark, and bodiless, but of great beauty and presence.

November 28, 1152
Feria [161]

 From Abbess Hildegard of St. Rupert of Bingen to the Marchioness von Stade: ‡‡*As you know, it has been the custom with us to celebrate the Requiem Mass at the time of burial, and on the 3rd, 7th, or 30th day following the death or burial. In consideration that the burial of your beloved daughter, Rikkarda, our Sister in Christ and lately elected Abbess of Bassum in the diocese of Bremen, fell on October 31, 1152, the day news reached our convent walls through a letter sent by her brother and your beloved son, Hartwig, archbishop of Bremen, we remembered her and all the faithful departed in the singing of the Office for the Dead in Matins early in the morning of Monday, November 3rd, while the night was still in its course.[162] In addition, we have celebrated today, since it is the 30th day after her death, the full Requiem Mass for the soul of the same dearly departed*

161. The term "feria" indicates all weekdays (a) to which there is assigned no fixed feast of the sanctoral (saints') cycle, (b) in Lent, (c) in the Octaves of Easter and Pentecost, or (d) of petition (rogation) or penance (ember).

162. As Jungmann points out (*Early Liturgy*, pp. 142–45), liturgical practices for dating memorials for the dead go back to the earliest days of the Church and are in fact pre-Christian and Oriental in origin, having to do with popular beliefs concerning the time that elapses between death and the separation of the soul. Since the Fathers of the Church were unsuccessful in expunging these beliefs, the commemorative days were Christianized: The third day is in keeping with the Resurrection, as is the seventh; the thirtieth recalls the number of days of mourning observed after the deaths of Moses and Aaron. We cannot be sure of exact dates for either the death or burial of Rikkarda, only that it occurred in the year 1152, and that certain preparations would have been required for the interment of an abbess. The journal proposes October 31st as the date of Rikkarda's death. The third-day commemoration would have fallen on

daughter. Fr. Volmar, whom you know, chanted the prayer at the Absolution, and I, the responsory, with the rest of the choir in full attendance, believing as we do in the strength of our combined prayers and the efficacy of sacramental Absolution for the aid of the soul of the departed. We also wish to inform you of our intention of dedicating to her our presentation of the Ordo virtutum, *a Play of the Virtues, concerning the journey of a soul, to be in our cloister church on the Feast of John the Evangelist, December 27, following the Office of Lauds and preceding the Mass of the day. We expect the prelates of Mainz and other official guests to be with us on that occasion, and your presence would be most welcome.*‡‡

(to be copied and sent on good vellum)

From Abbess Hildegard of St. Rupert of Bingen to Fr. Basel of St. Gereon: ‡‡ *Two varieties of beauty I send from the Requiem we celebrated today for Rikkarda—of sound and of sight. The bells were simply beautiful, three of my women pulling with all of their strength, and then having at one point to withhold and ground each other by the waist, as the momentum of those great clanging weights threatened to catapult them into the vault of the tower itself. For visual beauty, picture the steady light of twenty-two candles surrounding the empty catafalque, Volmar at the one end and I at the other. After the Absolution, I sang my responsory for a virgin, which you may not have heard, though it is an early one:* [163]

November 2nd, the Feast of All Souls, which was probably included in the calendar at St. Rupertsberg by that time, its observance having been regularized among the Benedictines by Odilo of Cluny in 1148; since in 1152 All Souls fell on a Sunday, the commemoration of Rikkarda and all the faithful departed would have been made on November 3rd.

⬛ 163. Traditionally, following the Requiem (Mass for the Dead), the celebrant and those serving him go to the bier, or to an empty catafalque if no body is present. A crossbearer stands at the head, the priest at the foot, where he delivers the prayer of Absolution; the cantor then intones the great responsory, *"Libera me"* (Deliver me). However, since the *"Libera me"*

You most glorious greenness,
You are rooted in the sun
And out of the dazzling brightness of the clearest day
You shine forth in a wheel
Which no earthly excellence comprehends;
You are encircled, embraced by the divine mysterium.
℣. *You blush like the dawn and you burn like a flame of the sun.*
You are encircled, embraced by the divine mysterium.[164]

I am content that her soul is planted among us. I ask that you join with us
for the performance, given in her memory, of the Ordo, *which we will give*
on the Feast of St. John the Evangelist, as planned.‡‡

(to be copied and sent on used vellum)

 I know the grace has been given to me to praise consecrated virginity in song, and I

begin to see the subtle varieties that can be achieved musically. We have done songs for the Virgin, for Ecclesia, and Sapientia. For Ursula's feast, we have this year done an entire set of narrative antiphons that tell the saint's life, with a hymn and two responsories for the offices of her feast day, and a long sequence for the Mass introduced through the heightened senses of Ecclesia.[165] The more I enter into the mystery of her vision, the more subtlety is required of the music as well as of the text.

was not fixed in this place until the 14th century (although it was used in the Office for the Dead), the use of Hildegard's own composition, a responsory common to virgins, seems appropriate. Its text, like those in place for the *Requiem*, is built around the themes of light and mystery, but adds the characteristic presence of greenness—perhaps even evergreenness—as an expression of Paradise. The mystical figure becomes a cosmic tree, then a burning bush, enflamed and illuminated by the orb of the sun.

▣ 164. *Lieder* #39, pp. 99–100.

▣ 165. "O Ecclesia, your eyes are like sapphire,/Your ears like the mountain of

When I write a hymn on this level of experience, it is not possible simply to repeat the music stanza after stanza, as most have done, because the text is always growing and changing. Nor is the form of the sequence as simple and straightforward as others may have it. In my sequence for St. Ursula, there may indeed be special inner relationships between each pair of half-strophes, but that relationship is never one of simple repetition. The more extended a piece becomes, the more complex the inner relationships. I see this more clearly as my Play of the Virtues grows towards completion: without any of the formal suggestions of liturgical pieces like responsory, antiphon, hymn, or sequence, its design and forward movement depend increasingly on the interplay between the developing text and its music. Now that we progress with the depiction of the sixteen Virtues and the Queen in the *Ordo virtutum,* I am challenged to discover further ways of varying the music in order to differentiate the many characters in a progressively dramatic confrontation of considerable length.

The life of St. Ursula is very much alive to me. It has been real in my heart since I first heard her noble story many years ago and learned about the community of virgins dedicated to her name in Cologne. Her history has existed in the *Sanctorale* of our tradition for as long as I have known it, and the ripening of my own spiritual understanding was the main prerequisite for praising her in new music. The genesis of the *Ordo* material is different. The idea of the struggle between the Devil, as the force of Evil, and the female Virtues first presented itself to me with the last of the *Scivias* visions. Until our arrival here at St. Rupertsberg, the material was visually rather flat, its sounds were sparse and dry. But our practice as a community in these extraordinarily demanding circumstances has given an outer habitus to the stark encounter. It has proved a real locus for fleshing out what was already there, only in skeletal form. As I was able to Bethel;/Your nose is a column of incense and myrrh,/And your mouth is the sound of abundant waters." (Opening stanza of sequence for St. Ursula.)

understand the Virtues in the way that the root meaning of the language so richly provides—not just as allegorical virtues as opposed to vices, but each one as *virtus*, a particular potency—their individual sensibilities began to emerge in my visions as their sounds caught my inner ear.

Although spiritual depth is always an issue in creation, my progress with the *Ordo virtutum* has been somehow more dependent upon the outer events of my human experience than were any of the liturgical songs. Once Basel had convinced me of the validity of notating the music that sang through me, once I had the opportunity to see as well as hear it, new possibilities suggested themselves having little to do with solmization, ecclesiastical modes, or the hexachords. A simple musical idea had its own shape, acquired a slightly different shape with simple variation, proliferated to take on yet a more elaborate shape, but still retaining within its new form the original germ. In the same way a kernel first receives moisture and soil, swells, and sends down roots, as a single pair of simple leaves emerge in the exact shape of the planted kernel. Next, pairs of leaves emerge (on a strengthening stem) that look quite different from the original pair, and finally buds and blossoms emerge among the leaves, blossoms all the while carrying in their centers the fruits that will replicate the shape of the original kernel. So the phrases of my melodies develop, all the while being modified by the suggestions of the particular words of the texts: if blood flows or water falls, the shape of the melody itself will be so informed. In the case of my new Magnificat antiphon for St. Ursula, emanating from the cascading of salvific blood from divinity through humanity, it is nearly as though the words of the text themselves paint the sounds in their own shapes.

Finally, there is for me a new understanding of the role of deepened earthly convictions, my loves and angers, admirations and disgusts. For so long I ignored them, tried to overcome them, became ill of them, trying to control them lest they betray or burst me with their strength. Now I see how they too can be tuned, powerful tools for Beauty. Nowhere has this been clearer than in the central song and response between Castitas and the Virtues,[166] a piece that grew out of my struggle to understand Rikkarda's seeming betrayal and the shock of her untimely death. My feeling now stands poised, transformed as the turning point of the entire play.

 Today Sr. Christina, one of the best among us, told me tearfully that my expectations are too high.

December 14, 1152
Third Sunday in Advent

I am too demanding; her instruction in the novitiate was not sufficient to handle the material I have given her to learn for the *Ordo virtutum*. It was not a case of disobedience. She simply broke down, and when I ordered a private conference with her during the afternoon, it all came pouring out. I had thought that giving her some scribal tasks would be good for all of us, keeping track of expansions I have made in the play as we approach the performance. Her skill with recording the music in neumes has sharpened as Basel has provided me with more ex-

166.

CHASTITY:

O Virginity, you remain within the royal chamber.
You burn with such sweetness in the embraces of the King
when the Sun irradiates through you so that your noble
*   flower never falls.*
O royal virgin, you will never know the shadow that fells the
*   dying flower.*

VIRTUES:

The flower in the meadow falls in the wind, the rain
*   splatters it.*
O Virginity, you remain in the music of the heavenly
*   subjects:*
you are the tender flower that never grows dry.

(From Hildegard's *Ordo virtutum*.) Since neither of these speeches from the 1180s Riesenkodex is found in any form in the Original *Ordo* material in the earlier *Scivias*, a persuasive argument can be made that Hildegard's exalted paean, whose promise of immortality is pictured in an image from the plant world that she knew so well, was part of her response to the death of Rikkarda.

amples of notation for her to see, and her facility to read texts has grown as well. It is not true that I expect all of them to be able to read before they are clothed with the habit, but they must be literate in our tradition, which means they must be capable of understanding the promises they make. They must have knowledge of the Rule and the psalms; the Vulgate must be their familiar, at least in the texts of the Office antiphons and the choral Propers we sing for Mass. In addition, I expect the choir nuns to have a strong desire for—if still burgeoning understanding of—what it means to enter into liturgical time, in order to be sure enough of a vocation before engaging with the bishop in the ancient Ceremony of the Consecration of a Virgin.

Perhaps my expectations are too high after all, for I think it not enough if we experience divinity only when we eat His body and drink His blood. The experience needs to be part of our own bodies: We must know the sanctity of the blood we ourselves shed. Nor is extreme fasting a correct practice, either as proof of piety, or as the assured pathway to union with the divine. Women who habitually starve themselves for days prior to the monthly Eucharist and fall into deep ecstasy when they receive the Host between their peeling, hungry lips should better attend to some balance in their lives. I would rather their contemplation included a deeper knowledge of their own bodies. They must know that one result of excessive fasting is to prevent the monthly flow of their own life-giving blood, making them brittle and dry, unreceptive to growth of any kind.

It is my intention that my professed nuns learn to step into the ever-

167. "O root of Jesse, who stands as the ensign of the peoples, before whom kings shall not open their mouths, to whom the nations shall pray, come to deliver us, tarry now no more." (Trans. Burlin, p. 41.) Of all the Old Testament prefigurations of Christ beloved by medieval theologians, miniature painters, and stained glass artists, none is dearer than the image of the royal lineage of patriarchs growing as a genealogical tree sprung from the loins of Jesse, father of David, whose final flowering is Christ. Its Biblical source is the prophecy in Isaiah 11.

present liturgical time with each of the eight sung offices; that we anchor ourselves there with each individual psalm, antiphon, and canticle we sing at each office, every day. And so we invoke the divine presence by singing directly to the holy ones. In our songs of praise, we address them as "you," not only as "he" or "she." When I write a sacred song for St. Disibode, for Wisdom, for Ursula, or for the Virgin, I both invoke their names and address them directly, just as in the great "O Antiphons" of Advent that lead us through the week preceding the Nativity. "*O radix jesse,*"[167] we sing, "*O domina mundi,*" "*O Sapientia,*" so that we step out of our own limited time into their ever-present time with our senses fully alive. Rather than starve ourselves, we must nourish ourselves to the task: In so doing, we help the ancient patriarchs and prophets beget Christ. We grow on the same sacred tree.[168]

The real problem for Christina is not her role as my musical scribe, but rather her singing of Castitas, a part conceived and nurtured with Rikkarda in mind. She doesn't know this, nor will I tell her. In the end, Christina will sing the role and sing it well, observing the seasonal loss of greenness as inevitable loss and renewal. It is I who grapple with the deeper meaning of loss, with an innocence no longer available, and of what is possible in its stead.

> *In the beginning all of creation was green*
> *and flowers bloomed in our midst;*
> *then the greenness fell.*
> *A Champion came into this, saw it, and said:*
> *"I am witness, but the golden number is not yet full.*
> *Behold the mirror of your Fatherhood:*
> *See how I carry the weariness in my flesh,*
> *how even my children lose heart."*[170]

What seems most im-possible is to let life come when our wounds are all

168. According to conventions of medieval Biblical exegesis, all Old Testament patriarchs prefigure in their persons, and prophets

stinking. I dread what more will be demanded, what else could be taken away, snatched from our care and the functioning of a whole community. How can we be open to grace, balanced, and stable, without protection from such deep wounds? I dread the return of those occasions when half my field of vision suddenly disappears, blackened and negated, torn from me as if out of its own existence. This makes me like those ignorant sailors who fear falling off the edge of the earth, as if the universe were a sharp-angled square rather than an egg.[169] Even I can see the rounded way things present themselves on the horizon as they approach our view.

> *Remember now that the fullness made in the beginnings*
>   *need not wither,*
> *that you have had the power*
> *never to yield your watch*
> *until you saw my body filled with buds.*
> *Now see how exhausted I am,*
> *how all my limbs fall into mockery:*
> *Father, I show you my wounds.*[170]

And the worst are the internal ones, those that threaten to fester because they have no outlet. To expose the wounds to the possibility of mockery means giving voice to the blood, allowing my blood to sing.

prophesy with their words, the coming of Christ. Hildegard's *Ordo virtutum* opens with

PATRIARCHS AND PROPHETS:
Who are those who look like clouds?

VIRTUES:
O holy ones of old, why do you marvel at us?
The word of God grows bright in the form of man,
and thus we shine with him,
building up the limbs of his beautiful body.

PATRIARCHS AND PROPHETS:
We are the roots, and you, the branches,
fruits of the living eye,
and grew up in its shadow.

Prayer and thanksgiving are impossible while my mind is so distracted with preparations for our presentation of the
Ordo virtutum on the Feast of St. John the Evangelist. Now that we are no longer under the protection and authority of Abbot Kuno at Disibodenberg, it is I, as abbess, who must take the full responsibility for deciding what it is we want to manifest as a community, and to whom. My intentions must be clear, whether or not they are supported by the archbishop. Each time I know I have created a situation in which my women must confront the world and its values—whether it is in the form of a retinue of clerics or a group of poor townspeople —I once more face the intertwining issues of enclosure and stability.[171]

Although in Christ there is nei-

169. Hildegard's conception of the universe during this period of her life is represented by a cosmic egg, which she described, physically and symbolically, in meticulous detail in Book I, Vision 3 of *Scivias* (its illumination strikingly reproduced in Führkotter, *Miniatures*, plate 4). The egg accounts for the precise origins of each of the four winds and the location of sun and moon, and places the earth (represented by the four elements) squarely in the center.

170. The Virtues quote their champion, Christ, who offers Himself in His bodily suffering as a living bridge between the consequences of the Fall and a renewed promise of the original Creation, when the golden number of time is fulfilled. The possibility of healing comes with His plea for our participation in His still-neglected mystical body.

171. Although it was not until 1298 that Pope Boniface VIII decreed universal enclosure for women, the practice had a long and sometimes inconsistent history. Particularly relevant to Hildegard's situation is a document of reform written by Idung of Prüfening, a 12th-century Cistercian monk in Germany. Beginning his argument for differences in the rule of enclosure for the two sexes with the usual premise concerning the relative weakness of women, he says, "the feminine sex...has four formidable and declared enemies. Two are within the sex itself: lust of the flesh and frivolous feminine inquisitiveness. Two are without: the casual

ther male nor female,[172] the fact is that the practice of enclosure is different for consecrated virgins than for professed monks, and St. Benedict did not address this issue in his Rule. We know what St. Paul, the Church Fathers, and Caesarius of Arles have said about the inherent weakness of women, and this would seem to require rules different from men. We know that, in the world, women's weakness makes them subject to violation by men, and their lack of education prevents them from teaching or otherwise exercising moral authority. But in Christ is neither male nor female; therefore our practice of perpetual virginity sets us apart from women in the world. Our vows should accord us certain strengths and privileges, opportunities for education, and appreciation of beauty. Surely, some women as well as men are called to go on pilgrimage. And I myself see that the time may

lechery of the masculine sex and the wicked envy of the devil. To these are added [the fact] that a woman can lose her virginity by violence—a thing which in the masculine sex nature itself prevents..." He goes further: "[Benedict] wrote no rule for consecrated virgins nor was it necessary to write any, because in those times monasteries of virgins existed only under the guardianship of abbots. And with good reason! It is not expedient for that sex to enjoy the freedom of having its own governance—because of its natural fickleness and also because of outside temptations which womanly weakness is not strong enough to resist." (Cited in Schulenberg, *Distant Echoes*, pp. 62–63.) Hildegard's solution to these problems and her insistence on autonomy are unique among the women as well as the men of her time. In fact, the women who were named heads of religious houses in the 12th century had considerably less power and autonomy than their counterparts in the 8th and 9th centuries. While it was still the decision of the abbot that determined the comings and goings of his monks, the same was not true for women, where bishops (and long-standing patristic prejudices) controlled and, in practical terms, precluded such determinations.

✦ 172. Galatians 3:28: "There is neither Jew nor Greek; there is neither bond nor free; there is neither male nor female: for you are all one in Christ Jesus."

come when I am called upon, not by the world, but from within, to teach by preaching to all others, men as well as women, in monasteries and cathedral chapters. Thus far, I have resisted such calls, as I have advised others to tend their own flocks, not because of enclosure but because of the promise of stability.

The Rule of St. Benedict is perfectly clear on the importance of stability. For Benedictines, the counsels of chastity and poverty are not sufficient for community. Stability is crucial. It is the promise that Rikkarda violated in going to another house, against my wishes and judgment. Not that living in a stable community is the only way to live a religious life, but it is the only way to do it as a Benedictine. From the earliest times, Christians have gone off to the desert to live eremetical lives of prayer; but I believe that living in community is of a higher order. Already in the 4th century, St. Jerome indicated this in his letter to Eustochium, which I read to my women.[173] He described the three different kinds of monks living in Egypt, for he was at that time a lone traveler, and he made it clear that those living in community, according to a rule, chose the better way. He himself lived a life of great service to the world, mastering strange languages, translating all we have of the word of God for our Vulgate Bible, was teacher of holy women and friend to educated widows—and ended his fruitful life leading a community of monks in Bethlehem.

Not only do we live together in a community, as did St. Jerome in the end, we also follow a Rule of great wisdom and moderation, conceived and written down by blessed Benedict of Nursia. The Rule we live by today first bound Benedict at Monte Cassino, and also his dear sister, St. Scholastica. It prescribes the order of our work, the *opus dei*, even the number of psalms we sing for each of the eight offices. It describes the nature of each job

173. Written in 384 from Rome and widely disseminated among medieval religious communities, Jerome's long letter is filled with historical information of the times as well as advice particularly directed towards women desirous of living a life committed to Christ.

I assign, whether cellaress, portress, prioress, or sacristan. It requires periods of total silence, the daily reading in the refectory as we eat. At the same time there remain some things not spelled out by St. Benedict. The abbot of each community must be the decision-maker for the issues that remain, and it is a part of why I insisted with such dogged certainty on leaving St. Disibode's with my women. Obedience to Abbot Kuno is no longer required of me, and when he asks me for liturgical songs for their patron saint, I do it out of charity, not obedience.

Although it is perfectly true that women are weaker than men, we are set apart in the religious life. Our vows protect us. We are not subjected to the rule of husbands, the mortal dangers of childbirth, or the physical terrors I see reflected in the frightened eyes of the townswomen of Bingen. As abbess, I am the arbiter for the issues not clarified by the Rule, and I depend for guidance on my understanding of the need for stability. In the case of Rikkarda, my obedience to the archbishop of Mainz was forced upon me in violation of that guide. In truth, there are still differences in the religious life for men and for women, and to sort them all out in detail would require that I write my own commentary on the Rule of St. Benedict.[174]

The complexity of these issues for an autonomous community of women like ours at St. Rupertsberg is nearly unprecedented, and, now that I hear rumors that full and absolute enclosure for women may be mandated by papal bull, I am of two minds. Enclosure for women has been a practice from the days of the earliest groupings of consecrated virgins. Understood from within, it protects our time and physical selves, our attention to contemplation, to learning and practicing psalmody, to singing praise, which is after all our vocation. Should it be imposed unilaterally from Rome, it could prevent our serving the bodies and souls

174. Hildegard did eventually write a commentary, occasioned by a request made of her by the Convent of Hunniensis. (*PL*, pp. 1053–66.) For a good English translation, see Feiss, *Vox Benedictina*, 7.2, pp. 117–58.

of both women and men. I fear some of the consequences. My own medical skills and spiritual gifts serve well those who climb the steep road to our gate. My need to physically oversee what our landholdings actually comprise, especially since we are so new, is not to be discounted. Last but not least, there are contacts that are sources of knowledge for us that require some regular comings and goings: inspired teachings of men such as Bernard of Clairvaux or Rupert of Deutz,[175] the long conversations I've shared with dear Basel of Cologne, who encourages me to notate my music and speak my prophecies to other communities.

We do not attend synods of bishops and abbots; we are already cut off from the possibility of sending representatives to visit foundations with great libraries or holdings of works of art. Letters are important links of communication, and eventually we need a working scriptorium within our own walls to copy what is most valuable, most beautiful, most elusive to remember. Like my visions. Is it ambition in me that so desires this possibility? My mind sometimes feasts on the thought—the powders, colors, inks from the East, the fragments of lapis and gold that could set down in gleaming illuminated paintings the experience that floods my mind in the Shadow of the Living Light. There is a way in which the experience is all wordless, and squeezing it into the thousands of words I pour forth sucks me dry.

O magnum mysterium![176] Tonight we celebrate the coming forth of our Savior through the

175. A Benedictine monk and theologian, Rupert (ca. 1075–1130), like Hildegard, ascribed his beginnings as a writer to direct visionary experience, although he himself had been formally educated at Liège and was well traveled early in life. In order to be insulated from a storm of criticism provoked by a thesis he wrote, Rupert spent time in the Rhineland at the monastery of Siegburg; there he came to the attention of the archbishop of Cologne, who was responsible for Rupert's election in 1120 as abbot of Deutz, a Benedictine monastery not far from Hildegard.

176. Responsory iv, Second Nocturn of Christmas Matins, is the only text on

royal gate, and it is my great joy that townspeople from Bingen can flock to our midnight Mass this year, that guests will arrive for the *Ordo* on the 27th. The consecration of our virginity is our sanctified power, our protection, and our opportunity to live educated, informed, spiritual lives. We can protect ourselves with walls of ritual that allow us to express our fervent longing for the rightful Bridegroom in sensuous color and song. So long as we live our lives in the spirit of *contemptus mundi*, it should not be necessary that physical walls of stone be builded by strangers. Let us be our own keepers of the gate.

 Until the first sounds of our singing—and even for a few seconds afterwards, until my concentration was entirely focused—I

December 27, 1152
Feast of St. John, Apostle
and Evangelist

expected to encounter the fierce gaze of Basel in the cloister church. I can only guess that his absence was due to some sudden incapacity; as recently as Christmas Day, I received his message assuring us how deeply he anticipated being with us for the *Ordo*, and how he was at the instant rejoicing with shepherds and all believers in the Great Mystery surrounding us. He of all people would most deeply have understood the complex perfection of the intertwining of religious celebration, particular feast, and climax of a particular Season in which the performance of the Play of the Virtues found its meaning. In the apocalyptic vision of John, the great war between Good and Evil manifests itself in the most cosmic terms—in seals, scrolls, beasts, and natural cataclysms far beyond rational imaging. And yet, unless one is truly the painter with the entire firmament for a canvas, or the angel floating in the empyrean who is privy to all the heavenly harmonies and to the spheres as well, that day to retain the characteristic opening that directly addresses the divine itself: "O great mystery and wondrous sacrament, that animals should see the newborn Lord lying in a manger: Blessed is that Virgin, whose womb deserved to bear Christ our Lord…"

such powerful visions as come from the Creator are as likely to strike us dumb, blind our eyes, seal our lips for ever after. The only remedy for those of us who wait zealously, our ears so painfully enlarged through Fear of God, is to be instructed in the grand design through the prologue to John's Gospel, as Basel emphatically reminded me, with some impatience, in conversation after conversation.[177]

I pray that his person is not in danger, and I deeply regret his absence at our performance today. What I could not have foreseen, but what finally became clear, is the extent to which each one became the Virtue she portrayed in the *Ordo virtutum*. More than anything else, it was in the nature of the music each woman sang, I think. I hadn't really planned it that way, for I only received what I heard with my inner ear; and, as I taught them, the constant stumbling and repeating precluded my being able to hear the consistency of the music for each. Humilitas, for example, sings the melodies most heavily embroidered: The decorations around the main tones are extremely complex and difficult to sing. On the other hand, no one could mistake the triumphant cry of Victoria just after the Virtues have bound Satan, because her long melisma on *"Gaudete"* [Rejoice!] lies high in the firmament and seems itself to set off the celebratory pealing of bells. The placement of the music for Castitas is entirely different; it lies much lower, yet her music has a more insistent quality than all the others, and within her narrow range of notes, relative to the other Virtues, it is she who most directly confronts the Devil.

And what a terrifying Devil Volmar turned out to be! Again, it is something no one could have guessed as I taught

177. The prologue to John's Gospel (1:1–18) teaches the eternal Word (Greek, *Logos*) through which all things were made and in which they live, tells how that Word became flesh in Christ, and how this Incarnation was introduced to humankind by John the Baptist. The prologue was intended to offer a translation from the things of heaven to the things of earth.

them their parts, since Volmar was, at the time, always attending to his own duties. He learned to speak his speeches with me, apart from my practices with the women, where my rendering of the Devil's speeches, in lowered voice, elicited nothing but embarrassed giggles. In the performing of it, we all recoiled visibly the first time he came thundering in at us with his accusations ending in the charge, "None of you even know what you are!"[178] The next time the Devil had a speech, I prepared myself for what was coming and was better able to observe how it affected others. There were gasps from everyone, including the visiting prelates of Mainz. Volmar had a way of spitting out his first few words, and, in so doing, almost tearing through the last tones of the singer he followed. It was as though he were physically leaping out of darkness to pounce upon the sweet sounds of his intended victims. He overlapped the melodies of the Virtues the way we do in our antiphonal singing, giving a sense of urgency, then taking all kinds of pauses, slowings-down, and even real stops within his

178. From the first scene, and throughout the play, the Devil persistently taunts the Virtues with a lack of consciousness and self-knowledge, to the point that their identity becomes a major leitmotif. After nearly 800 years' neglect, the *Ordo* is now recognized as the earliest known morality play, unique in its conception, its use of through-composed original music, and its presentation of the Devil as the only male and nonsung role. While some theorize that the *Ordo* was first performed at the dedication of the cloister church at Rupertsberg on May 1, 1152, I believe it more consistent with a whole view of her work and life to locate the play within the liturgical year. Since the play specifically concerns the apocalyptic struggle between good and evil, this strongly suggests liturgical placement in the Advent-Parousia cycle. The fact that the most eloquent spokeswoman for the Virtues is Chastity indicates that Hildegard has taken this opportunity to develop her belief about the role of sanctified virginity in the struggle against evil in her own time—which she may well have understood as "the last times," by dint of the corruption and decadence against which she preached and taught.

own delivery. In the end, the Devil enhanced the courageousness of the Virtues by erupting so stormily with each vicious attack.[179]

But nothing was more startling than the two piercing upward leaps in the incipit of the last chorus of the Virtues. Those who could manage the intervals—exceeding the span of the diapason in a way no one had heard sung in music before—were nearly ecstatic in its accomplishment.[180] The chorus of Virtues is not for the fainthearted, and I believe the experience of doing the *Ordo* was ennobling for us all. We have much more of a sense of community for having done it, and, true to the Season of the Parousia, we have been tested and not found wanting.

 I pray that his person is not in danger. Basel has been in my prayers at every office and continually in between, and I realize how much his absence from the performance yesterday alarmed me. Months ago, at the time when he had recovered sufficiently to leave our dispensary, it somehow didn't occur to me to realize at what depth our friendship had taken root. Even with Volmar, whose loyalty and service have never failed but only grow, whose being radiates warmth, constancy, and concern, the friendship is not this way. At

December 28, 1152
Sunday after the Nativity and Feast of the Holy Innocents

179. After the Virtues have bound Satan and proclaimed victory, the Devil is addressed by Chastity: "In the mind of the most high, Satan, I trod your head under my foot [Gen. 3:15], and, in virginal form, I nurtured a sweet miracle wherein the Son of God came into the world...." Even though bound, Satan hurls his last taunt at Chastity: "You don't even know what it is you nurture, because your womb is devoid of the beautiful form received from a man, in this way you go against God's command of sweet intercourse; therefore you know not what you are." Chastity replies, "I brought forth one man, who through His very birth gathers up all of human nature to Himself, against you."

180. This figure, consisting of two ascending perfect

times, especially when Basel and I have talked about music—indeed, once when he was most ill and we sang the psalms of Vespers together in the dispensary—there has been an urgent, probing quality in the air between us that generates its own heat and energy. His cheironomic hand is a marvel and makes my listening new, and when he leads me in singing or sings a liturgical piece himself in example, the line of melody never flags and each word of text is as if painted in air with the shapes of its neumes. The beauty of mystery is loved equally between us; although he claims never to have seen with his inner eyes the scenes I describe, he recognizes their beauty immediately and senses the depth from which they are sourced.

How well he understands my impatience with most people's eagerness to reduce deep mystery to its most trivial details. For years now, the excitement about Ursula and her virgin martyrs has grown more superficial, and most of it emanates from the sale of relics unearthed by the thousands in the cemetery near the Church of St. Ursula. Having lived for so long in Cologne, Basel hears it all—the distractions to which people fasten their thoughts: Why the large femurs if there were no men among the group? And, if there were holy men who went out of respect as protectors, how could the virgins have remained chaste? They point to the tiny bones that were dug up, skeletal parts of infants, babies born of the virgins of Ursula, they charge. How the "faithful" love the scandalmongering, and how effectively it keeps them from noticing the pathetic failures of their own priests, the buying and selling of ecclesiastical positions, the maneuvering of the secular powers to gain control over those Church offices, not excepting even that of the bishop of Rome.

We have spoken about the fifths in succession, is repeated once more in the next verse; these ninths, in addition to being extremely difficult to sing, break every known modal structure. Given the placement of these leaps, and the contrasting nature of the strikingly low placement and conjunct movement of the melody of Chastity which precedes it, the effect is strikingly dramatic.

mysterious qualities of true relics. The basis of belief must be the Incarnation, the embodying of the Word, as in the prologue to John's Gospel. Eternal divinity embodied in bones—the Light of the World buried in flesh, taking root in a heart, mind, and spirit to move among those longing for a sign—is a great power. Miraculous healings occur; people understand, see, and listen for the first time. Buried in the altar, the bone is alive, as well as the piece of wood of the cross brought to serve in our Mass, as part of our celebration of the inner life. Basel says that the bones of the Theban martyrs create such a golden glow that the air in the north chapel of St. Gereon's is colored as if in the glow of the full moon.

But the corruption and selfishness of the present cathedral hierarchy is just as real as the moonlight. There are six priests whose duties have little to do with serving the flock and whose personal abuses are obvious to any who would dare to look through the armor of the offices they use to protect themselves and deceive the rest of the world, for their concern for the eyes of the world is the force that drives them, not any inner light or love of God. They abbreviate their offices, until their singing of divine praise is a mere token and may be only mumbled rather than sung. Basel the cantor, instead of being liturgical servant of the glorious melodies praising God in this cathedral, becomes less and less important. One after another the priests scurry into private chapels to say offices, even to say private, devotional Masses as well, for a price; the body of Christ, the voice and corporate building of that body in sung praise, becomes a sham.

His pain at abuse and deceit is great, I am sure, but when the abuse turns inward, he loses his ability to distinguish inner from outer. Since the first time he arrived at our door, he has been brought back in a litter once, and once tied to the saddle by a friend. His woman companion serves him no longer, for she has chosen to stay with us. It surprises me that he has never opposed her decision; first, that he honored her right to make the decision, and second that he has never resented our taking her from him. Although it is clear to me that it is the Mother of God whom she serves in all she does, and not ourselves, in the case of lay sisters it is easy to understand that human wishes and needs may intervene. Basel has never indicated anything to me but respectful acceptance of her life with us and hears with apparent pleasure the reports I have made at her ever-growing competence in attracting new swarms of bees for our honey and wax candle supply, her instinctive skills with training the sweet peas on trellises, and her ingenuity at devising new methods of drying and preservation of harvested fruits.

So he wrestles the demons without her, and it is horrible when he plunges into the abyss. Once it was so severe that all four of his limbs jerked as if convulsing, each one out of harmony with the other. For a night and a day, he had no control over his poor body: constantly and uncontrollably he voided his gut, and the dehydration made his thirst unquenchable. I had water and weak broth administered hourly, and feared he would bite off his tongue with the strength of the terrible shudderings. When such breakdowns occur, the deep link between us disappears, the rare experience of equality between man and woman becomes impossible, for his dependence is total: his music-making hands are useless, his intuitive powers blinded, and his confusion like that of an obstinate, belligerent child.

We pray and God heals, but not having access to his deep soul has been the greatest sorrow for me at such times. I pray that his person is not in danger.

 This day was nearly balmy. One of those singular January days when the unbroken sound of water dripping **January 6, 1153**

Feast of the Epiphany

from all the eaves reminds me that the angle of the sun has changed, the light is stronger: The light of the world is manifest today. ‡‡*Begotten before the daystar, and before all ages, the Lord our Savior is this day made manifest to the world.*[181] ‡‡

181. First antiphon at Vespers on Epiphany.

Even before Lauds—awake before dawn—I puzzled over teaching them how to understand the two highly compressed texts about three miracles. I anticipated they would ask about the three miracles in the antiphon for the Benedictus at Lauds:

> *This day is Ecclesia united to the heavenly spouse,*
> *For Christ, in the Jordan, washes away her sins:*
> *The Magi run to the royal nuptials with gifts,*
> *And the guests of the feast are gladdened by the water*
> *turned into wine, alleluia.*

And so I read to them in the refectory from Jerome. Volmar and I had earlier discussed the highly compressed nature of the texts of the most important antiphons for today, and we had agreed that he would use an Epiphany sermon of Augustine for the Mass that would shed some light on both the Benedictus antiphon and the one for the Magnificat at Second Vespers:

> *We celebrate a holy day adorned by three miracles:*
> *This day, a star led the Magi to the manger:*
> *This day, water was changed into wine at the marriage-feast:*
> *This day, Christ vouchsafed to be baptized by John in the*
> *Jordan, for our salvation, alleluia.*

But the explanations were all so much words: mine, Volmar's, even St. Jerome's and St. Augustine's. We all betray our experience of the divine, if we fail to convey that "In the beginning was the Word" is neither the word as it appears so beautifully on the page, nor the word polished rhetorically and delivered from the pulpit. It is the word coming into being, even the capacity of the word to come into being.

So much for exegesis. It hardly mattered anyway, because what they really asked this morning—the few who bothered—was not about those three separate epiphanies made present today in liturgical time.

They asked about the miracle of the three kings, by which they meant the nature and meaning of gold, frankincense, and myrrh. Simple and solid, I thought, and all of my teaching for naught; but I should not have been so disappointed or surprised. After all, why not? Why water into wine? Why not ice dripping into water? Brown turning to green? Night becoming day? Like plants, we take in water and sun, and grow. Or we don't. Over this liturgical year, our cloister church has miraculously materialized, manifest from stone, wood, shapes of arches, proportions of certain ratios to amplify certain configurations of sound. And we ourselves have brought forth new songs of praise and will continue to grow and change and bring forth fruit. Or not.

After Compline

Some nights I find myself speaking wearily to a woman carved in wood. I call her Ursula. I think of her that way, not merely as a nameless statue whose origins are unknown to me. She sustains me with her presence: for my part, I often rail and gnash my teeth as well as pray; but her mode is silence. She is wonder itself, a tree transformed.

I do not share her with anyone; she is the guardian of my private quarters, and my comfort is in that molded silence. Her knee is just slightly bent, not in obeisance, but to show the curve of energy in repose. Her face and whole stretch of high forehead are not shrouded by her habit; rather the head comes forward, emerging lucent blossom from sepaled layers of her nunlike veil, and waits. Her throat, the calyx, is wrapped, supported by the winding vine of limbs. She waits to sing the word.

> *A sculptor took such care to wrap your head*
> *In swaddling clothes,*
> *Protect the fecund swarming thoughts and sightings,*
> *Shelter head from icy blasts and scalding sun:*
> *I know you for a world.*

Chronology of Hildegard's Life
1153–1179

Before
1158

According to the preface to her second book of visions, which she began in the year 1158 and called *Liber vitae meritorum* (Book of Life's Merits), Hildegard had in the eight years since the completion of *Scivias* set down and completed two medical works, *Physica* (nine sections describing the properties and medicinal uses of herbs, trees, stones, and the elements, the qualities of fish, birds, beasts, reptiles, and metals) and *Causae et curae* (a descriptive compendium of diseases and their cures). She had also produced for her community a body of liturgical songs and the sung morality play. During her lifetime, the songs were arranged into a cycle which she called *Symphonia harmoniae celestium revelationum* (Symphony of the Harmony of Celestial Revelations), and she sent them in manuscript to at least one other community, a group of monks in Villers.

1158–
1163

In spite of recurrent illness, Hildegard made three long journeys to various religious communities in the Rhineland, where she preached at cathedrals and monasteries. She also completed the second book of visions and began her third and most cosmological book of visions, which she called *Liber divinorum operum* (Book of Divine Works). This was completed about 1174.

1163

Emperor Frederick Barbarossa, known to Hildegard in person and through correspondence, issued an edict of protection to St. Rupertsberg in perpetuity.

1165

Hildegard founded a daughter house at Eibingen, across the Rhine from St. Rupertsberg.

1170   After another period of debilitating illness which lasted for several years, Hildegard made a fourth preaching tour, to the south, into the dukedom of Swabia.

1173   Volmar died; greatly at loss, Hildegard eventually obtained the services of the monk Gottfried, who began writing Hildegard's *Vita*, a biography interspersed with autobiographical segments.

1176   Gottfried died, and the monk Guibert of Gembloux, already a correspondent and a great admirer of Hildegard, came to serve as her secretary from 1177 until the end of her life.

1178   Hildegard and her nuns were denied the right to sing the liturgy by the prelates of Mainz for refusing to exhume the body of a man buried in the cemetery at Rupertsberg. According to Hildegard, he had been reconciled to the Church after excommunication. The canons disputed his reconciliation and the conflict became a butt of clerical politics. Finally, in desperation, Hildegard wrote an impassioned letter to the prelates of Mainz about the function of music as humanity's bridge to the heavenly harmonies, and how the Devil tries to prevent the adoration of God by silencing music sung in His praise. In a carefully worded theological argument, she placed the prelates of Mainz squarely on the side of the Devil.

1179   The interdict was lifted in March, and Hildegard died on September 17 that year, at the age of eighty-one.

Translations of the Ursula Songs

Divine Office AT MATINS FOR THE VIGIL OF HER FEAST
Responsory: Spiritui sancto honor sit

Honor the Holy Spirit,
Who gathered in the mind of the virgin Ursula
A virginal flock like doves.
Like Abraham she set out,
Leaving her homeland behind,
And just for the loving embrace of the Lamb,
She broke from her chosen betrothed.
℣. In fact, this army of purest gold
Crossed over the sea
With free-flowing virginal hair.
But who has ever heard of such things?
And just for the loving embrace of the Lamb,
She broke from her chosen betrothed.
℣. Glory be to the Father and to the Son
And to the Holy Spirit.
And just for the loving embrace of the Lamb,
She broke from her chosen betrothed.

FOR THE BENEDICTUS CANTICLE AT LAUDS OF THE VIGIL
Antiphon: O rubor sanguinis

O royal redness of blood,
You flowed down from a high place
Which divinity has touched;
You are the flower that winter never damaged
With the freezing blast of the Serpent.

AT MATINS FOR HER FEAST
Responsory: Favus distillans

A dripping honeycomb
Was the virgin Ursula,
Who longed to embrace the Lamb of God.
Honey and milk under her tongue,
Because she gathered to herself
A fruit-bearing garden and the most fragrant flowers
In a swarm of virgins.
℣. *Therefore, Daughter of Zion, rejoice*
In this most golden dawn!
Because she gathered to herself
A fruit-bearing garden and the most fragrant flowers
In a swarm of virgins.
℣. *Glory be to the Father and to the Son*
And to the Holy Spirit.
Because she gathered to herself
A fruit-bearing garden and the most fragrant flowers
In a swarm of virgins.

FOR THE PSALMS AT VESPERS AND LAUDS
Antiphon: Studium divinitatis

Devotion to Divinity
Bestowed the Kiss of Peace
Upon the virgin Ursula and her flock
In highest praise.

Antiphon: Unde quocumque venientes
And so wherever the travelers went
They were received with the joy of heavenly paradise,
Because their way of life so honorably
Manifested the love of God.

Antiphon: De patria etiam earum
From their native land and also from other regions,
Monks and philosophers joined with them
Who kept their virginal custody
And who ministered to them in all things.

Antiphon: Deus enim in prima muliere
God presignified
In the first woman
That the Woman should be nourished by the care of the Man.

Antiphon: Aer enim volat
Even the air flies
To exercise its office
Among all creatures,
And the firmament sustains the air,
And the air is nourished by this kind of strength.

FOR THE MAGNIFICAT CANTICLE AT FIRST VESPERS
Antiphon: Et ideo puellae istae

And for this purpose
These same young maidens
Were sustained by the greatest Man,
Becoming a detachment of troops
To the Royal Descendant in their virginal nature.

For the Benedictus Canticle at Lauds
Antiphon: Deus enim rorem in illas misit

Next God sent into the maidens the fertilizing moisture
Out of which their many-faceted reputation grew so much
That all people shared this respectful fame
Like food.

For the Magnificat Canticle of Second Vespers
Antiphon: Sed diabolus in invidia sua

But the Devil in his envy
Jeered at such a thing;
Not a single work of God did he leave intact.

At Vespers and Lauds for her Feast
Hymn: Cum vox sanguinis

When the voice of the blood of Ursula and her innocent flock
Resounded before the throne of God,
The ancient prophecy from the Plain of Mambre
Quickened through the root in a true showing of the Trinity,
And it said:
    "This blood of yours touches us,
    So let all of us rejoice."
After that the flock for the Lamb appeared
In the form of a ram hanging in the brambles,
And it said:
    "Let there be praise in Jerusalem
    Shining through the crimson of this blood."
Next came the sacrifice of the calf,
Which the old law revealed to be a sacrifice of praise,
Clothed about with rainbowed light,
That light which hid the face of God from the prophet Moses,
Uncovering only His back.
In this way there are priests
Who reveal God through their own tongues,

Although they are not able to see Him fully.
And they said:
> *"O most excellent flock,*
> *This virgin who on earth is called Ursula*
> *Is named in highest heaven Columba,*
> *Because she gathered to herself an innocent flock."*

O Ecclesia, you are praised in such a flock.
This great flock,
Like the bush not consumed by fire that Moses had seen,
Telling us that their God had planted her in the primal root
Which in ourselves He had formed out of clay,
Intending she live on without marriage to a man,
Shouted out in the most brilliant voice,
A sound of purest gold,
Of topaz, and of sapphire, all clothed about with gold.
Now let all of heaven rejoice,
And all the earth be honored in that rejoicing.
Amen.

At Mass   *Sequence:* O ecclesia, oculi tui
O Ecclesia, your eyes are like sapphire,
Your ears like the mountain of Bethel;
Your nose is a column of incense and myrrh,
And your mouth is the sound of abundant waters.
In a vision of true faith
Ursula loved the Son of God;
She abandoned her espoused along with the world
And gazed into the sun,
And she called to the fairest young Man, crying out:
> *"With great yearning*
> *Have I longed to come to you*
> *And to sit at your side*
> *For the heavenly wedding feast,*
> *To stream towards you in a strange way,*
> *Like a cloud which streams sapphire in the purest air."*

And after Ursula had so spoken,

Popular opinion spread among all people everywhere.
And the men said,
> *"The innocence of this ignorant girl!*
> *She doesn't know what she's talking about!"*

And they began to make fun of her
In great swells of harmony
Even up to the time when the burden of bearing the fire
Fell upon her.
Then everyone came to recognize
How defiance of the world is like the mountain of Bethel.
They even identified that sweetest fragrance of incense and myrrh,
Because defiance of the world surpasses all perfumes.
Then the devil fell into his own members
Who slaughtered in those graceful bodies
The noblest way of life.
And all the elements heard this wrenching cry
And themselves cried out before the throne of God:

> "Watch! *the crimson blood of the innocent Lamb*
> *Is poured out in abundance with her marriage pledge.*
> *Let all the heavens hear this*
> *And with consummate music let them praise the*
>   *Lamb of God,*
> *Because the throat of the ancient Serpent*
> *Is strangled in those pearls*
> *Who express in matter the Word of God."*

Bibliography

Antiphonaire de Hartker, MSS Saint-Gall 390–91. In *Paléographie musicale,* Series II, Vol. I. Berne: Éditions Herbert Lang, 1970. Facsimile of tenth-century rhythmic chant manuscript containing text and musical neumes for the whole Divine Office.

Antiphonaire monastique, Codex F.160 de...Worcester. In *Paleographie musicale,* Vol. XII. Berne: Éditions Herbert Lang, 1971. Facsimile of thirteenth-century manuscripts with text and music for the Office.

Antiphonale sarisburiense. Ed. Walter Howard Frere. London: Plainsong & Medieval Music Society, 1925. Six volumes. Facsimile of thirteenth-century manuscripts containing Office chants for Salisbury Cathedral.

Aquinas, Thomas. *Summa theologica.* Ed. Roland Potter. London: Blackfriars, 1969.

Bagnall, Anne D. *Musical Practices in Medieval English Nunneries.* Ann Arbor: University Microfilms International, 1979.

Bible. Translated from the Latin Vulgate (Douay-Rheims). Baltimore: John Murphy, 1914. (Occasionally other English translations have been used in this book.)

Biblia sacra iuxta vulgatam versionem. Stuttgart: Württembergische Bibelanstalt, 1975. Two volumes. It was the Latin Vulgate translation of the Bible that Hildegard knew and that is the basis for the English translations used herein.

Blackley, R. John. *Music for Holy Week,* Vols. I & II. L'Oiseau-Lyre 417 324–2 OH and 425 114–2 OH2. Recordings of chants mainly from tenth-century MS Laon 239.

———. "Rhythmic Interpretation of Chant." In *The Hymnal 1982 Companion.* Vol. I. Ed. Raymond Glover. New York: Church Hymnal, 1990. Pages 238–52.

Bradshaw, Paul F. *Daily Prayer in the Early Church: A Study of the Origin and Early Development of the Divine Office.* New York: Oxford University Press, 1982.

Breviarium monasticum. Mechlin: H. Dessain, 1950. Four volumes.

Breviarium romanum. Turin and Rome: Marietti, 1949. Four volumes.

Burlin, Robert B. *The Old English Advent: A Typological Commentary.* New Haven: Yale University Press, 1968.

Ceremony of the Consecration of a Virgin. Ed. Benedictines of Regina Laudis. Bethlehem, CT: Regina Laudis, 1949. Cf. *Monastic Ritual* and *Rituel monastique.*

Codex Albensis. Budapest: Akademiai Kiado, 1963. Facsimile of twelfth-century manuscript containing texts and neumes for the Office.

Corpus antiphonalium officii. In *Manuscripti 'Cursus romanus,'* Vol. I. Ed. René-Joanne Hesbert. Rome: Herder, 1963.

Dronke, Peter. "The Composition of Hildegard of Bingen's *Symphonia.*" In *Sacris erudiri* XIX, 1969–70, pp. 381–93.

———. *Fabula: Explorations into the Uses of Myth in Medieval Platonism.* Leiden and Cologne: E. J. Brill, 1974. Chapter 2.

———. *The Medieval Poet and His World.* Rome: Edizione di Storia e Letteratura, 1984. Essays: "Tradition and Innovation in Medieval Western Colour-Imagery," pp. 55–104, and "The Beginnings of the Sequence," pp. 115–44.

———. *Ordo virtutum*. Deutsche Harmonia mundi 1C 165–99 942/43 T. Translation of play included with recording.

———. *Poetic Individuality in the Middle Ages: New Departures in Poetry 1000–1150*. Oxford: Clarendon Press, 1970. Chapter 5 contains a critical edition of the text of Hildegard's *Ordo virtutum*.

———. "Problemata hildegardiana." In *Mittelalteinisches Jahrbuch* 16, 1981, p. 107–131

———. *Women Writers of the Middle Ages: A Critical Study of Texts from Perpetua (d. 203) to Marguerite Porete (d. 1310)*. Cambridge: Cambridge University Press, 1984. Chapter 6.

Dunn, E. Katherine. "French Medievalists and the Saint's Play." In *Medievalia et humanistica*, NS 6, 1975, pp. 51–62.

Flanagan, Sabina. *Hildegard of Bingen: A Visionary Life*. London and New York: Routledge, 1989.

Le Graduel de St-Denis. Paris: Nouvelles Éditions Latines, 1981. Facsimile of eleventh-century manuscript with texts and chant neumes for the Mass Propers.

Graduale sarisburiense. Ed. Walter Howard Frere. London: Plainsong & Medieval Music Society, 1894. Facsimile of thirteenth-century manuscript containing Mass Proper chants for Salisbury Cathedral.

Hildegard von Bingen. *Opera omnia*. In *Patrologia latina*, Vol. 197. Ed. J.-P. Migne. Paris: J.-P. Migne Editorem, 1855. The orginal Latin of most texts written by Hildegard.

———. *Scivias*. Trans. M. Columba Hart and Jane Bishop. New York: Paulist Press, 1990.

———. *Hildegard of Bingen's Scivias*. Trans. Bruce Hozeski. Santa Fe: Bear and Co., 1986.

———. *Hildegard of Bingen's Book of Divine Works*. Ed. Matthew Fox. Santa Fe: Bear and Co., 1987.

————. "Hildegard von Bingen: Explanation of the Rule of St. Benedict." Intro. and trans. Hugo Feiss. In *Vox benedictina,* 7:2.

————. *The Miniatures from the Book Scivias—Know the Ways—of St. Hildegard of Bingen from the Illuminated Rupertsberg Codex.* Commentary by Adelgundis Führkotter, trans. Hockey. Turnhout, Belgium: Brepols, 1977.

————. *Hildegard of Bingen Symphoniae harmoniae caelestium revelationum: Dendermonde St.-Pieters & Paulusabdij MS. Cod. 9.* Intro. Peter van Poucke. Peer, Belgium: Alamire, 1991. Facsimile of music manuscript written ca. 1175.

————. *Hildegard von Bingen: Lieder.* Ed. Pudentiana Barth, M. Immaculata Ritscher, and Joseph Schmidt-Görg. Salzburg: Otto Müller, 1969. Transcription of texts and the music for all the songs. Cf. Ritscher, M. Immaculata: *Kritischer Bericht zu Hildegard von Bingen: Lieder.* Salzburg: Otto Müller, 1969.

————. *Symphonia.* Intro. and trans. Barbara Newman. Ithaca: Cornell University Press, 1988.

————. "Five Liturgical Songs by Hildegard von Bingen (1098–1179)." Intro. and trans. Barbara Lachman Grant. In *Signs,* Vol. 5, No. 3, Spring 1980.

————. *Hildegard von Bingen: Ordo virtutum.* Ed. Audrey Ekdahl Davidson. Kalamazoo: Medieval Institute, 1985. Transcription of text and music.

————. *Ordo virtutum: Hildegard of Bingen's Liturgical Morality Play.* Intro., text, and trans. Bruce William Hozeski. Ann Arbor: University Microfilms International, 1979.

Holy Week Chant. Tournai: Desclee, 1961.

Illich, Ivan, and Sanders, Barry. *The Alphabetization of the Popular Mind.* New York: Random House, 1989.

Jungmann, Josef A. *The Early Liturgy: To the Time of Gregory the Great.* Trans. Francis A. Brunner. Notre Dame: University of Notre Dame Press, 1959.

————. *The Mass of the Roman Rite: Its Origins and Development.* Trans. Brunner. New York: Benziger, 1951, 1955. Two volumes.

Klauser, Theodor. *A Short History of the Western Liturgy: An Account and Some Reflections.* Trans. John Halliburton. Oxford: Oxford University Press, 1979. Second edition.

Kraft, Kent Thomas. *The Eye Sees More than the Heart Knows: The Visionary Cosmology of Hildegard of Bingen.* Ann Arbor: University Microfilms International, 1978.

Liber usualis. Tournai and New York: Desclee, 1963. Edition of chants for the Mass and much of the Office prepared by the Benedictines of the Abbey of Solesmes.

Martin, Rebecca. *Textiles in Daily Life in the Middle Ages.* Cleveland: Cleveland Museum of Art, 1985.

Mitchell, Sabrina. *Medieval Manuscript Painting.* New York: Viking Press. 1964.

The Monastic Ritual for Nuns of the English Benedictine Congregation. Ed. The Benedictines of Stanbrook. Worcester: Stanbrook Abbey Press, 1961.

Murbach, Ernst. *The Painted Romanesque Ceiling of St. Martin in Zillis.* Ed. with photographs by Peter Heman. New York: Frederick A. Praeger, 1967.

Neuls-Bates, Carol, ed. *Women in Music: An Anthology of Source Readings from the Middle Ages to the Present.* New York: Harper & Row, 1982.

Newman, Barbara. *Sister of Wisdom: St. Hildegard's Theology of the Feminine.* Berkeley: University of California Press, 1987.

Offertoriale triplex cum versiculis. Ed. Karl Ott and Rupert Fischer. Solesmes: Abbaye Saint-Pierre de Solesmes, 1985. Contains texts and music for the Mass Offertories with their ancient verses.

Page, Christopher. *Sequences and Hymns by Abbess Hildegard of Bingen.* Hyperion A 66039. Notes and translations included with recording.

Bibliography

The Passion of Saint Ursula [Regnante domino]. Trans. Pamela Sheingorn and Marcelle Thiébaux. Toronto: Peregrina, 1990.

Price, Lorna. *The Plan of St. Gall in Brief*. Based on the work by Walter Horn and Ernest Born. Berkeley: University of California Press, 1982. Architectural witness to life in a medieval monastery.

Le Prosaire de la Sainte-Chapelle (vers 1250). Macon: Protat, 1952. Facsimile containing texts and music for sequences.

Rituel monastique propre aux moniales de langue française de l'Ordre de Saint Benoît. Dourgne: Abbaye Sainte-Scholastique, 1974.

Roman Breviary in English. New York: Benziger, 1951. Four volumes.

Roman Missal ("Knox Missal"). London: Burns and Oates, 1961.

Rule of St. Benedict. Latin and English, ed. Timothy Fry. Collegeville: Liturgical Press, 1981.

————. Trans. Anthony C. Meisel and M. L. del Mastro. Garden City: Doubleday, 1975.

Sacks, Oliver. *Migraine: Understanding a Common Disorder*. Berkeley: University of California Press, 1985. Chapter 3.

Schmitt, Miriam. "Blessed Jutta of Disibodenberg: Hildegard of Bingen's Magistra and Abbess." In *American Benedictine Review* 40:2, June 1989.

Schnapp, Jeffrey. "Virgin Words: Hildegard of Bingen's *Lingua ignota* and the Development of Imaginary Languages Ancient to Modern." In *Exemplaria* 3:2, October 1991.

Schulenberg, Jane Tibbets. "Strict Active Enclosure and Its Effects on the Female Monastic Experience (500–1100)." In *Distant Echoes* (Cistercian), Vol. 1, ed. John A. Nichols and Lillian Thomas Shank, 1984.

Seward, Desmond. *Monks and Wine*. New York: Crown, 1979.

Bibliography

Vita sanctae hildegardis. Trans. Anna Silvas. Published in 4 parts in the Arcadia, Australia, periodical *Tjurunga* 29 (1985), 30 (1986), 31 (September 1986), and 32 (May 1987).

Singer, Charles. *From Magic to Science: Essays on the Scientific Twilight.* New York : Boni & Liveright, 1928. Chapter 6.

Taft, Robert. *The Liturgy of the Hours in East and West.* Collegeville: Liturgical Press, 1986.

Talley, Thomas J. *The Origins of the Liturgical Year.* New York: Pueblo, 1986.

Weiser, Francis X. *Handbook of Christian Feasts and Customs.* New York: Harcourt, Brace & World, 1958.

Wiethaus, Ulrike. "Cathar Influences in Hildegard of Bingen's Play 'Ordo virtutum.'" In *American Benedictine Review* 38:2, June 1987.

𝔇𝔦𝔰𝔠𝔬𝔤𝔯𝔞𝔭𝔥𝔶

A Feather on the Breath of God: Sequences and Hymns. Gothic Voices, Christopher Page. Hyperion A66039 (CD and LP).

Geistliche Musik des Mittelalters und der Renaissance. Instrumentalkreise Helga Weber. LP: TELDEC 66.22387.

Gesänge der hl. Hildegard von Bingen. Schola der Benediktinerinnenabtei St. Hildegard in Eibingen, M. I. Ritscher. LP: Psallite 242/040 479 PET.

Hildegard von Bingen und ihre Zeit. Ensemble für frühe Musik Augsburg. CD: Christophorus 74584.

The Lauds of Saint Ursula. Early Music Institute, Thomas Binkley. CD: Focus 911.

Music for the Mass by Nun Composers. University of Arkansas Schola Cantorum, Jack Groh. LP: Leonarda LPI 115.

Ordo virtutum. Sequentia. Harmonia Mundi CD: 77051-2-RG; LP: 1C 165-99 942/43 T.

Symphoniae, Geistliche Gesänge. Sequentia, Barbara Thornton. Harmonia Mundi CD: 77020-2-RG; LP IC 067-19 9976 I.

Zwei Geistliche Gesänge. Schola der Benediktinerinnenabtei Rüdesheim-Eibingen. 45 rpm: Psallite 138/250 973 PEX.

Glossary of Liturgical Terms
for the Twelfth Century

Terms are alphabetically arranged, except for portions of the Divine Office, the Mass, and the liturgical Seasons, which are arranged separately and in order of occurrence under those three headings.

ANTIPHON   (Greek "sounding against") Brief text taken from the Psalms (or sometimes from the Gospels) sung before and after a psalm in order to interpret it in terms of the day's feast.

BENEDICAMUS DOMINO   (Latin "Let us bless the Lord") Versicle sung by the cantor at the conclusion of hours of the Divine Office; followed by the response *Deo gratias* ("Thanks be to God").

BREVIARIUM   (Lat. "short") Single- or multivolume book containing the whole of the Divine Office (otherwise spread across various cantorial and choral books, and lectionaries).

CANTICLES   New Testament songs found in the Divine Office—at Lauds (the Canticle of Zachary, father of John the Baptist: "Blessed be the Lord, the God of Israel") and at Vespers (Mary's Magnificat: "My soul doth bless the Lord, and my spirit rejoices in God my savior").

CANTOR/CANTRIX   The chief solo singer of the *schola cantorum,* frequently its director as well.

COMMON OF SAINTS   Propers of the Mass and Divine Office that may be used for certain categories of saints (e.g., apostles, martyrs, confessors).

DEACON   Main assistant to the liturgical celebrant at the altar.

Glossary of Liturgical Terms

DIVINE OFFICE Structures of antiphons, psalms, lessons, responsories, hymns, and prayers sung eight times or "hours" daily; extends the liturgical presence of the Mass. The hours, according to their Latin names and with translations, in order:

> MATINS The "morning" liturgy, correctly sung in the dead of night, consisting of the Invitatory and a hymn, with three Nocturns. Each Nocturn typically consists of an antiphon with three psalms followed by three lessons, each having its responsory.
>
> LAUDS The dawn "praise," consisting of antiphons and psalms, a hymn, canticle, and the prayer of the day.
>
> PRIME Sung at the "first" of the hours of the day, 6 A.M. First of the so-called Little Hours, each basically having a hymn, an antiphon with three psalms, and prayers.
>
> TERCE Sung at the "third" day-hour, 9 A.M.
>
> SEXT The "sixth," noon.
>
> NONE The "ninth," 3 P.M.
>
> VESPERS The "evening" hour, sung at the time of the lighting of the lamps against the darkness; similar to Lauds in form.
>
> COMPLINE The hour of "completion," in the dark, before retiring; always the same three psalms (no antiphon), a hymn, and prayers.

EUCHARIST (Gr. "giving thanks") Another name for the Mass of the Faithful, sometimes used simply to refer to the presence of Christ in the form of bread.

HYMN Postscriptural poem set to music, popular in its sentiment and rhythmic appeal.

INVITATORY Vulgate Psalm 94, which, with an antiphon recurring after each verse, begins each day's Divine Office: "Come, let us rejoice unto the Lord, let us shout with joy to the Rock of our salvation."

KALENDARIUM (based on Lat. "calling") Formal listing by month and date of the feasts of the temporal and sanctoral cycles.

LESSON Reading from the Old or New Testament at Mass (the Epistle) or Divine Office.

LITURGY Formal, traditional actions of thankful worship performed by or in the name of a religious community.

MASS Liturgical presence and reenactment of the death and glorification of Christ, ending in a communion with Christ in the form of bread and wine. Divided into the Mass of the Catechumens, for those studying the faith, similar in its readings and prayers to the Jewish synagogue service; and the Mass of the Faithful, for baptized initiates. The parts of the Mass, in order:

> INTROIT (from Lat. "entrance") Processional antiphon from the Proper of the feast sung with a psalm by the *schola cantorum.*

> KYRIE ELEISON (Gr.) "Lord, have mercy. Christ have mercy. Lord have mercy." Each petition is sung three times by the congregation; the first part of the Ordinary of the Mass.

> GLORIA IN EXCELSIS DEO (Lat.) "Glory to God in the highest," Ordinary chant based on the song of the angels to the shepherds at Christmastide.

> COLLECT Prayer from the Proper for the feast, sung by the celebrant.

> EPISTLE Proper reading from the New Testament.

> GRADUAL (Lat. "step," wherefrom at the altar the cantor originally sang this chant) Proper response to the Epistle.

> ALLELUIA (Hebrew "praise Yahweh") Proper psalm verse with Alleluias sung by cantor or cantrix and *schola* to accompany the procession preceding the Gospel.

> TRACT Ancient, ornate psalm verses sung in Proper chant by the *schola*; replaces the Alleluia during times of penance or mourning.

SEQUENCE   A sort of hymn, popular in nature, whose Proper text and melody move in strophic pairs; sung by the *schola*, it extends the Alleluia on certain feasts.

GOSPEL   Proper reading from one of the four evangelists, Matthew, Mark, Luke, or John, sung by the deacon.

CREDO   (Lat. "I believe") Ordinary statement of beliefs, sung by the congregation; concludes the Mass of the Catechumens.

OFFERTORY   Proper processional antiphon sung by the *schola* as bread, wine, and gifts are brought to the altar; a portion of the antiphon is repeated after each of one to four ornate solo verses. Begins the Mass of the Faithful.

PRAEFATIO AND SANCTUS   (Lat.) Celebrant-sung "bridge" with thrice-"Holy" Ordinary chant sung by the congregation, connecting the Offertory to the Canon.

CANON   (Lat. "law") The most sacred, unchanging part of the Mass, read by the celebrant in lowered voice.

PATER NOSTER   (Lat. "Our Father") The Lord's Prayer, Ordinary chant sung by the celebrant.

AGNUS DEI   (Lat. "Lamb of God") Ordinary chant petitioning mercy and peace, sung by the congregation.

COMMUNION   Proper antiphon sung by the *schola* in alternation with psalmody; accompanies the procession for the receiving of communion.

ITE MISSA EST   (Lat. "Go, you are dismissed") Versicle sung by the deacon at the conclusion of Mass, to which all respond *"Deo gratias"* (Thanks be to God).

MISSALE   (Lat.) Altar book containing all the texts (and some or all of the music) for the Mass.

OCTAVE   Eight-day celebration of a major feast.

Glossary of Liturgical Terms

OFFICE *See* Divine Office.

OPUS DEI *See* Divine Office.

ORDINARY Those parts of the Mass or Office that are, relatively speaking, unchanging; sung by the celebrant and the entire congregation. (See Mass and Divine Office.)

PAROUSIA (Gr. "arrival") The final coming of Christ, celebrated during the Advent/Epiphany liturgical Season at the end of the temporal cycle. (*See* Seasons.)

PRAYER The main prayer for the day's feast, used at Mass and also in the Office at Lauds, Terce, Sext, None, and Vespers.

PROCESSION Liturgical movement of celebrant, *schola cantorum*, and/or the congregation, accompanied by song.

PROPER Those parts of the Mass or Divine Office that change according to the feast being celebrated; sung by the celebrant, deacon, or *schola cantorum*. (*See* Mass and Divine Office.)

PSALMS Old Testament book of 150 songs that are the basis of Catholic liturgy. Psalmody or the singing of psalms has its origins in the Jewish temple and synagogue.

RESPONSE (℟.) Answer to a versicle, sung by the congregation.

RESPONSORY Proper response sung by the *schola* to a lesson, usually verses of a psalm; its form is characterized by a reprise of a portion of its text and music.

SANCTORAL CYCLE The sum of the feasts celebrating the lives or martyrdoms of holy persons.

SCHOLA CANTORUM (Lat. "school of singers") Small group devoted to the study and singing of liturgical music, especially the chant Propers.

SEASONS Time-portions of the temporal cycle, in order:

> ADVENT At once the beginning and the ending of the liturgical cycle,

the one anticipating the coming of Christ into the world at Christmas and the other His final coming at the end of the world (*Parousia*). It begins on the fourth Sunday preceding Christmas.

CHRISTMAS   Celebration of the birth of Christ; December 25th through January 5th.

EPIPHANY   The manifesting of Christ (a) to people after His birth and (b) to humankind at the end of time; from January 6th.

LENT   (From the Old English "long"); five and one-half weeks of penitential practices culminating in the recollection of Christ's death and burial on Good Friday and Holy Saturday.

EASTER   Celebration of Christ's resurrection and ascension into heaven.

PENTECOST   Celebration of the coming of the Holy Spirit to the apostles and disciples of Christ and the continued work of that Spirit throughout history. Begins fifty days after Easter, lasts until Advent.

TEMPORAL CYCLE   The sum of the feasts celebrating the mysteries of Christ's life, divided into liturgical seasons.

VERSICLE   (**V.**) Phrase or sentence sung by the celebrant, deacon, cantor, or cantrix answered by an equally brief response from the congregation.

About the Author

BARBARA LACHMAN is a teacher of the Alexander Technique and a writer who has for twenty years immersed herself in the life and music of Hildegard of Bingen. Recently returned from codirecting La Casa del Libro, a library-museum in San Juan, she lives in Baltimore with chant medievalist John Blackley and enjoys the frequent company of two grown children. She continues to write and give seminars about Hildegard.

Other Bell Tower Books

The pure sound of the bell
summons us into the present moment.
The timeless ring of truth
is expressed in many different voices,
each one magnifying and illuminating the sacred.
The clarity of its song resonates within us
and calls us away from those things which often distract us—
that which was, that which might be—to That Which Is.

BEING HOME: A BOOK OF MEDITATIONS
by Gunilla Norris
*An exquistie modern book of hours, a celebration of mindfulness
in everyday activities.*
Hardcover 0-517-58159-0 (1991)

NOURISHING WISDOM: A NEW UNDERSTANDING OF EATING
by Marc David
*A book that advocates awareness in eating and reveals how our attitude
to food reflects our attitude to life.*
Hardcover 0-517-57636-8 (1991)

Sanctuaries: The Northeast
A Guide to Lodgings in Monasteries,
Abbeys & Retreats of the United States
by Jack and Marcia Kelly
The first in a series of regional guides for those in search
of renewal and a little peace.
Softcover 0-517-57727-5 (1991)

Grace Unfolding: Psychotherapy in the Spirit
of the Tao-te ching
by Greg Johanson and Ron Kurtz
The interaction of client and therapist illuminated through
the gentle power and wisdom of Lao-tzu's ancient Chinese classic.
Hardcover 0-517-58449-2 (1991)

Self-Reliance: The Wisdom of Ralph Waldo Emerson
as Inspiration for Daily Living
Selected and with an introduction by Richard Whelan
A distillation of Emerson's essential spiritual writings
for contemporary readers.
Softcover 0-517-58512-X (1991)

Compassion in Action: Setting Out on the Path of Service
by Ram Dass and Mirabai Bush
Heartfelt encouragement and advice for those ready to commit time
and energy to relieving suffering in the world.
Softcover 0-517-57635-X (1992)

Letters from a Wild State: Rediscovering Our True
Relationship to Nature
by James G. Cowan
A luminous interpretation of Aboriginal spiritual experience applied t
o the leading issue of our time: the care of the earth.
Hardcover 0-517-58770-X (1992)

SILENCE, SIMPLICITY, AND SOLITUDE: A GUIDE FOR SPIRITUAL RETREAT
by David A. Cooper
This classic guide to meditation and other traditional
spiritual practice is required reading for anyone contemplating a retreat.
Hardcover 0-517-58620-7 (1992)

THE HEART OF STILLNESS: THE ELEMENTS OF SPIRITUAL PRACTICE
by David A. Cooper
How to deal with the difficulties that can arise in meditation, both on retreat and at
home— a companion volume to Silence, Simplicity and Solitude.
Hardcover 0-517-58621-5 (1992)

ONE HUNDRED GRACES
Selected by Marcia and Jack Kelly
With calligraphy by Christopher Gausby
A collection of mealtime graces from many traditions, beautifully
inscribed in calligraphy reminiscent of the manuscripts of medieval Europe.
Hardcover 0-517-58567-7 (1992)

SANCTUARIES: THE WEST COAST AND SOUTHWEST
A GUIDE TO LODGINGS IN MONASTERIES, ABBEYS
& RETREATS OF THE UNITED STATES
by Marcia and Jack Kelly
The second volume of what the New York Times *called*
"the Michelin Guide *of the retreat set."*
Softcover 0-517-88007-5 (1993)

BECOMING BREAD: MEDITATIONS ON LOVING AND TRANSFORMATION
by Gunilla Norris
A book linking the food of the spirit—love—with the food of the body—bread.
More meditations by the author of Being Home.
Hardcover 0-517-59168-5 (1993)